BUDGET MASTER'S

$SAVINGS GUIDE$

Melodie Moore

Publications International, Ltd.

Melodie Moore is the editor and publisher of the monthly newsletter *Skinflint News* and writes newspaper and magazine columns about money-saving ideas. She is a former Certified Public Accountant who devotes her time to teaching others about how to achieve a frugal lifestyle. For more information on *Skinflint News,* you can write to P.O. Box 818, Palm Harbor, Florida 34682-0818.

8 7 6 5 4 3 2 1

ISBN: 0-7853-3884-5

TABLE OF CONTENTS

FALL

Fall's a good time to gear up for savings. The air conditioning gets turned off, and you'll get a break before the heater has to be turned on. Use the tips in this chapter to see just how low your power bill can go.

Fall also means back-to-school time. If you're not careful, the back-to-school season can empty your wallet and max out your charge cards. But don't worry—in this chapter you'll find ways to save when you send the kids back to school. Halloween and Thanksgiving are coming up, too—but the holidays don't have to be expensive. Low-cost treats will make the holidays fun.

BACK-TO-SCHOOL SAVINGS

About a month before school starts, discount, drug, and grocery stores will have back-to-school sales. The stores will typically offer one or two items at cost or even below cost to get you in the door. They hope you will pick up the door-buster sale item and also buy all the rest of your supplies there (at regular prices, of course). Before school starts, stock up on the bargains and wait to buy any other needed supplies later.

Typical Back-to-School Sales

When school starts, teachers will give students a list of required supplies. Some of these lists include everything from an outdated slide rule to colored glue and stickers! Wait to buy any unusual supplies until your child's teacher requests that the students bring them in. If a teacher is planning a special project that requires additional supplies, he or she will let students know when to bring the supplies. If you buy all the

SCHOOL SUPPLIES	Regular price	Sale price	Savings
Pencils (10)	$.99	$.80	$.19
Notebook paper (100 sheets)	1.19	.90	.29
Folders (each)	.79	.60	.19
Composition books (75 pages)	1.29	.90	.39

school supplies on the "required" list, you could spend close to $100, and chances are good that many of the supplies will not be used—or that the teacher will get them as a donation from a local business.

Look for good buys on office supplies that you use around the house. Many times index cards, envelopes, and writing paper go on sale during the back-to-school blitz. Stock up!

Don't buy expensive book covers. Look around the house for something to use as a book cover. Paper grocery bags, newspaper comics, leftover wallpaper, or even old posters make great book covers. The kids will love their "designer" book covers.

Clothes

Just like school supplies, socks and underwear can be on sale at bargain prices during the back-to-school season. Stock up on socks and underwear for the entire family during the terrific back-to-school sales.

CHEAPER IN THE BOYS' DEPARTMENT	Girls' dept.	Boys' dept.	Savings
Basic T-shirt	$8.99	$6.99	$2.00
Elastic-waist shorts	7.99	4.59	3.40
Windbreaker jacket	18.99	12.99	6.00
Total cost and savings	$35.97	$24.57	$11.40

Brands compared may be different, but basic style and quality are the same. Prices are from a single week in 1995.

If you have several small children, buy basics that can be passed down to either sex. Red and blue shorts or T-shirts are perfect for either boys or girls. To make a hand-me-down from an older brother look more feminine, sew some lace on the collar or pocket or around the sleeves.

Older children will need to have clothes like their peers' to help them fit in. Self-esteem is very important for preteens and teenagers; they need to pick out their own clothes. At this age it is a good idea to give them a certain amount of money and let them pick out exactly what they want to wear. As long as the clothes are modest and socially acceptable, try not to be critical of their choices. Let your children learn to shop and stay within a budget.

Look for T-shirts, shorts, jackets, and other accessories for girls and young women in the boys' and men's departments. These items will almost always be much cheaper in the boys' department than similar items in the girls' or juniors' department.

The only food that never goes up in price is food for thought.

Anonymous

Lunch-Box Bargains

You can save about 50 percent on lunch costs by packing your children's lunches with inexpensive items. A lunch box filled with prepackaged snacks and other expensive foods will quickly cost more than the price of a school lunch.

Low-cost sandwiches include turkey, tuna, bologna, egg salad, peanut butter and jelly, and leftover meat such as pot roast or chicken. Other frugal lunches include leftovers such as chili, spaghetti, goulash, or

FRUGAL LUNCH

The Wrong Way to Pack a School Lunch

	Cost
Roast beef sandwich	$1.00
Pudding cup	.25
Prepackaged potato chips	.32
Animal crackers (individual box)	.89
Juice box	.37
Total	$2.83

The Right Way to Pack a School Lunch

	Cost
Peanut butter and jelly sandwich	$.22
Popcorn	.10
Homemade brownie	.08
Carrot sticks	.05
Juice made from concentrate	.08
Total	.53
Savings	$2.30
Average cost of elementary school lunch	$1.25

soup. They can be reheated in a microwave or packed in a thermos.

Homemade or store-brand cookies, fresh fruit in season, vegetable sticks (cut yourself, of course), crackers, popcorn, and homemade brownies make good inexpensive additions to the lunch box. Make lunch-box cupcakes by putting the frosting in the middle instead of on top.

Prepackaged individual bags of crackers, chips, or cookies are very expensive per ounce. Buy potato chips, cookies, and other lunch goodies in large bags or boxes and repackage them into just the right amount for your child.

Plastic bags used for chips and cookies can be used several times. Have your child bring home the lunch box or bag with the plastic bags inside so you can decide whether to use them again or toss them.

Instead of buying expensive drink boxes for lunches, put their favorite drink into a plastic container with a lid. (Some margarine tubs are perfect for a drinking glass, since they are tall and slim.) Freeze the drink, if it's noncarbonated, to keep it cold until lunchtime.

Cure for the Back-to-School Blues

When school starts, most children will also begin after-school activities such as sports or lessons. Make friends with the other parents that go to the same events; work out a car-pool schedule to give you more time and save gas.

Call around to local eye clinics to see if any offer free vision testing for school-age children. Many clinics offer a once-a-year free vision screening during the back-to-school season.

THE FRUGAL PUMPKIN PATCH

Even if you don't have little ones in the house, Halloween wouldn't seem right without a pumpkin to carve. Here are a few ways to make Halloween fun and frugal.

Buy a pumpkin from a local pumpkin patch. Most of the cost of a pumpkin comes from shipping, which causes damage. At a pumpkin patch, you'll be likely to find the best pumpkins, save money, and have fun picking out your own pumpkin.

For inexpensive holiday candleholders, use tiny pumpkins, squash, or apples. Just carve a hole in the top for the candle.

Jack-o'-Lantern

A fresh pumpkin will keep well outdoors for weeks if it doesn't freeze, but once carved, it's very perishable. After carving, rub the cut areas of a jack-o'-lantern with petroleum jelly to help make it last longer.

Cut a hole in the bottom of the pumpkin just large enough to hold a small flashlight. Carve the pumpkin as usual, but instead of buying lots of candles, just flip on the flashlight. This makes it fun for small children to light the pumpkin. A flashlight is much safer than candles and is less expensive in the long run.

Using the Pumpkin Meat

You can get the most out of your pumpkin by using it to make pumpkin bread or freezing the pumpkin to make a Thanksgiving pumpkin pie. To keep the inside fresh, your first option is to not carve the pumpkin but to instead draw a jack-o'-lantern face on your pumpkin with black markers. This looks fine during the day, but it's not as much fun at night. If you want to carve your pumpkin and eat it too, wait until the last minute (Halloween afternoon or the day before Halloween) to carve your pumpkin. Save all the pieces cut out during the jack-o'-lantern carving. When the little ones are finished trick-or-treating, bring the pumpkin inside. Cut the pumpkin into pieces, remove the skin, and toss away any blackened or bruised pieces. Grate the fresh pumpkin and try it in your favorite recipe for pumpkin bread.

To save the inside of a jack-o'-lantern for pumpkin pie, remove the skin and cut the pumpkin into small pieces. Boil in a covered pan of water until pieces are soft. Drain off water and puree the pumpkin in a blender or food processor until it's smooth. Freeze the mashed pumpkin until Thanksgiving. Thaw and substitute the canned pumpkin in your favorite pumpkin pie recipe with the same amount of fresh pumpkin.

Use the Inside, Too

Don't throw away the pumpkin seeds. They make a tasty, inexpensive snack. Just rinse the seeds, mix with butter and seasonings, and toast them in the oven.

Toasted Pumpkin Seeds

2 cups seeds
1½ tablespoons butter or oil
1½ teaspoons salt
¼ teaspoon garlic powder (optional)

Rinse seeds until clean. Remove all strings. Spread seeds on a clean towel and pat dry. Toss with melted butter or oil, salt, and garlic powder. Spread on ungreased cookie sheet. Bake at 250 degrees until light brown (about 20 to 25 minutes).

SAVE BIG ON ENERGY COSTS

SAVE BIG ON ENERGY COSTS

Heating and cooling your house is the largest energy expense (it makes up 46 percent of residential energy used by Americans), but you can significantly reduce your energy costs in many ways. Most utilities offer low-cost or no-cost home energy audits to help you identify where your house could be wasting energy and costing you money. Give your local utility company a call and find out what services it has available. Some utilities will even help pay for energy-saving improvements.

Here are some ways to save energy (and $$$) around the house.

Heating Water

About 15 percent of all the energy the average American family uses in the home goes toward heating water. Don't waste it. Do as much household cleaning as possible with cold water. Always turn off the hot water first, then turn off the cold water.

Repair leaky faucets promptly to save water and the costs of heating the water.

Use cold water rather than hot to operate your food disposer. This saves the energy needed to heat the water and aids in getting rid of grease. Grease solidifies in cold water and can be ground up and washed away.

If you need to rinse dishes before putting them in the dishwasher, use cold water.

Install a water-saving device, or aerator, in your kitchen sink faucet and all shower heads. They are inexpensive to buy; some utilities will even give them to you free of charge. By reducing the amount of water in the flow, you use less hot water and save the energy that would have been required to heat it. The lower flow pressure is hardly noticeable.

When you replace your water heater, it is especially important to look for an energy-efficient model. It may cost a little more initially, but you'll quickly start saving money. An energy-efficient water heater can save you about $160 per year if you have an electric water heater.

Get in the habit of taking short showers instead of baths. It takes about 30 gallons of water to fill the average bathtub. A shower with a flow of 3 gallons of water per minute uses only 15 gallons in 5 minutes. Assuming you use half hot and half cold water, you can save more than 7 gallons of hot water each time you take a shower instead of a bath.

Refrigerators and Freezers

About 15 percent of all the energy Americans use in their homes goes to refrigerators and freezers. When you are forced to replace these items, shop for an energy-efficient model.

Make sure your refrigerator door seals are airtight. To test refrigerator door seals for energy leaks, close the refrigerator door over a dollar bill so it is half in and half out of the refrigerator. If you can pull out the dollar easily, the latch may need adjustment or the seal may need replacing in order to conserve energy and reduce your electric bill.

Don't keep your refrigerator or freezer too cold. Efficient temperatures are 38 to 40 degrees for the fresh food compartment of the refrigerator and 5 de-

FROZEN ASSETS

Is a separate freezer worth the extra energy costs? On the plus side:

Buy in bulk: Stock up and save when meats and frozen foods are bargain-priced.

Cook in quantity: Double the recipe and freeze one for later or cook several meals at one time and freeze until needed.

Save the garden surplus: Freeze the extra bounty for later in the year.

Eat at home: With a full freezer, you won't be tempted to eat out, which will result in a substantial savings.

The downside: Electricity to operate a freezer manufactured before 1986 costs approximately $144 per year for a frost-free model and approximately $80 for a manual-defrost model. If you have a freezer made after 1986, a frost-free model will cost about $80 per year to operate and a manual-defrost unit will cost about $43 to operate.

Keep in mind that it is cheaper to operate one larger refrigerator instead of a smaller refrigerator and a separate freezer.

A separate freezer is very convenient, and if you use it wisely it can help you save money instead of costing more money. Another bonus is that when an unexpected expense, such as a large car-repair bill, comes your way, you can temporarily lower your grocery bill by eating the bargains you have stored in the freezer. This will help you get through the cash-flow crunch without having to use your credit cards.

grees for the freezer section. A deep freezer for long-term storage should be set at 0 degrees.

Think twice before you keep an old refrigerator around as a spare. Unless you really need the additional refrigerator space, it probably will cost more energy than it is worth. An older frost-free refrigerator costs about $128 per year to operate.

Lighting and Appliances

Operating lights and household appliances accounts for 24 percent of the energy the average American family uses in the home.

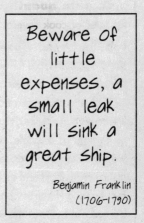

Beware of little expenses, a small leak will sink a great ship.

Benjamin Franklin
(1706-1790)

Many utilities offer much lower rates during the off-peak hours. Try to use such energy-intensive appliances as dishwashers, clothes washers and dryers, and electric ovens in the early morning or late evening hours to help reduce peak load energy use. Find out when your utility company offers the lowest rate, and take advantage of the savings.

Use kitchen, bathroom, and other ventilating fans wisely. In just one hour, these fans can blow away a houseful of warmed or cooled air. Be sure to turn them off as soon as they have done their job.

When you buy a new appliance, look for the highest Energy Efficiency Rating (EER). The higher the number, the less it will cost you to operate. Buying an energy-efficient appliance may cost a bit more initially, but that expense will quickly be recouped in reduced operating costs. Appliances manufactured before 1986 are not energy-efficient.

THE LIGHT SIDE OF FRUGALITY

Switch to compact fluorescent lights. Compact fluorescent lights can fit into many incandescent-lamp sockets and provide the same quality of light. The compact fluorescent lamps are three to four times as efficient as conventional lightbulbs and last ten times as long. For example, an 18-watt compact fluorescent bulb provides the same amount of light as a 75-watt incandescent bulb. You may have to swallow hard over the extra money to buy these bulbs, but the savings in electricity costs will pay for the compact fluorescent bulb in about a year.

Higher-wattage incandescent bulbs are more efficient than lower-wattage bulbs. It takes two 60-watt bulbs to provide as much light as a single 100-watt bulb. By using one higher-wattage bulb in a fixture that holds several bulbs, you'll get just as much light and use less electricity. (Follow directions on the lighting fixture about maximum wattage, and leave burned-out bulbs in the other sockets for safety's sake.)

When buying lightbulbs, look for energy-efficient ones available from the major lightbulb manufacturers. They use 5 to 13 percent less energy than standard bulbs. They probably will cost slightly more than regular incandescent bulbs, but the extra cost is more than made up in energy savings.

Halogen bulbs offer an even greater savings than the energy-efficient lightbulbs, and they last longer. The purchase price will be higher, though.

Keep lighting fixtures clean. Clean bulbs and fixtures will produce more light for the same amount of money.

Remember, doing a lot of little things to reduce your power bill will add up to big savings. Most of these tips are painless and easy; a few require you to spend a little money now to save a lot of money later.

Cooking

In the kitchen, keep electric and gas stove-top burners and reflectors clean. They will reflect the heat better, and you will save energy. When you have a choice, use the stove top rather than the oven. If you have them, use small electric pans or toaster-type ovens for small meals rather than an electric oven. They use much less energy. Microwaves and pressure cookers can save energy, since they take less time to cook the food.

If you need to buy a gas oven or stove, shop for one that has an automatic electronic ignition system instead of pilot lights. This one option will save a significant amount of gas.

If you cook with electricity, get in the habit of turning off the burners and oven several minutes before the cooking time is up. The heating element will stay hot long enough to finish cooking without using more electricity.

Watch the clock or set a timer instead of opening the oven door to check on food. Every time you open the door, heat escapes. More energy will be needed to cook your food.

Dishwasher

According to the U. S. Department of Energy, the typical dishwasher uses 14 gallons of hot water per load. It's important to use it energy-efficiently. Be sure your dishwasher is full without being overloaded when you turn it on. Choose the air-dry setting on

SAVE WITH ENERGY-EFFICIENT APPLIANCES	*Average Annual Cost to Operate*		
	Pre-1986 appliance	**New appliance**	**Money saved per year**
Air conditioner (central)	$320	$160	$160
Air conditioner (window unit)	64	43	21
Clothes washer	96	48	48
Dishwasher	75	48	27
Freezer (frost-free)	144	80	64
Freezer (manual-defrost)	80	43	37
Refrigerator	128	75	53
Range (electric)	64	53	11
Range (gas)	45	35	10
Television	27	11	16
Water heater (electric)	320	160	160
Water heater (gas)	160	130	30

Figures assume an electricity price of 8 cents per kilowatt hour and a gas price of 60 cents per therm. Operating costs for clothes washers and dishwashers include the cost of water heating.

your dishwasher to save energy. If you don't have an automatic air-dry choice, turn off the control knob after the final rinse and prop the door open slightly to speed the drying time.

If your dishwasher has a rinse-and-hold cycle for soiled dishes, keep this in mind: This cycle uses an additional 3 to 7 gallons of hot water each time you use it. You'll save money by thoroughly rinsing dishes by hand in cold water instead of running the rinse-and-hold cycle.

Laundry

Don't use too much detergent when washing clothes. Oversudsing not only wastes detergent, it also makes your washing machine work harder and use more energy. Presoak heavily soiled garments in cold water. You'll avoid two washings and save energy.

Most of us know to keep the lint screen in the dryer clean, but you also need to keep the outside exhaust of your clothes dryer clean. Check it regularly. A clogged exhaust lengthens drying time and increases the amount of energy used.

Save energy needed for ironing by hanging clothes in the bathroom while you're bathing or showering. Many times, the steam will remove the wrinkles so you won't have to use the iron. You'll save both time and energy!

FALL BEST BUYS CALENDAR

Knowing when to buy is one smart strategy for saving money. Buying fruits and vegetables in season helps lower your annual grocery bill. Month after month you can stretch your budget by shopping the sales. Many retailers still stick to traditional sale dates. This best-buys calendar for fall lets you know in advance when to look for specific items. By timing your purchases, you can save thousands of dollars each year.

September

Beef, beets, broccoli, cauliflower, chicken, clams, corn, eggplant, fish, grapes, peaches, pears, peppers, plums, scallops, tomatoes, housewares, hardware, garden supplies, children's clothes, automobiles, bathing suits, car batteries, dishes, mufflers, paint.

October

Apples, beans, beef, beets, broccoli, Brussels sprouts, cauliflower, chestnuts, cranberries, parsnips, pears, pork, pumpkin, scallops, sweet potatoes, turkey, turnips, winter squash, women's winter clothes, hosiery, lingerie, major appliances, silverware, camping equipment, glassware, school supplies.

November

Apples, beef, broccoli, Brussels sprouts, cauliflower, chestnuts, cranberries, fish, lamb, oranges, oysters, pears, pumpkin, sweet potatoes, tangelos, tangerines, turkey, turnips, winter squash, blankets, dresses, water heaters, men's shoes, women's fall clothes.

SAVE LOADS ON LAUNDRY COSTS

The cost of keeping clothes clean can quickly add up. Here are some tips to keep the high cost of cleaning clothes down.

You'll save energy by doing one large load instead of two small or medium loads. Some newer washing machines are considered large-capacity machines. These large-capacity machines allow you to wash bigger loads and save energy. When you need to replace a washing machine, a large-capacity model will save you money. It may cost slightly more, but it will quickly save money in energy consumption.

Don't Wash in Hot Water

When washing clothes, conserving hot water is the key to saving, since studies show that 90 percent of the cost of washing clothes is attributable to the expense of heating the water. If you have an electric hot water heater, you can save up to $230 per year by washing clothes in cold water. With a gas water heater, you can save up to $60 per year if you switch to cold water. Use hot water only for sheets and towels or for heavily soiled clothes that have been presoaked. Always rinse with cold water. Remember that the temperature of the rinse cycle does not affect cleaning power. A cold-water rinse for laundry not only saves energy, but it reduces wrinkles, too!

Turn down the thermostat on your water heater. Most water heaters are preset at 140 degrees, but a setting of 120 degrees is perfectly adequate for most household needs. When you reduce your hot water temperature, you will save money washing in warm and hot water. A lower thermostat temperature also reduces the risk of a family member getting burned by hot water.

FABRIC SOFTENER FOR LESS
Fabric softener dryer sheets are convenient, but they also can be expensive. Dip a sponge in liquid fabric softener diluted with an equal amount of water. Simply toss the squeezed-out sponge in the dryer along with your load of clothes to be dried. The sponge will work just like a fabric softener sheet for a fraction of the price.

If you have a dishwasher without a booster heater, lowering the thermostat to 120 degrees is not recommended. The machine needs water at 140 degrees to do a good job of killing germs. You can find out if your dishwasher has a booster heater by reading the instruction manual (you did save it, didn't you?). When buying a new dishwasher, you'll save money over time if you buy one with a booster heater. The dishwasher will cost about $30 extra, but you'll quickly save that by being able to lower the thermostat on your water heater.

Avoid the Wash-Day Blues

Instead of buying an expensive all-color bleach product, try adding either ½ cup of white vinegar or ½ cup of baking soda to the wash load. Either one will help clean and brighten clothes. And both are priced right!

If clothes need presoaking, put clothes, detergent, and water in the washing machine, let it stand for sev-

SAVE LOADS ON LAUNDRY COSTS

THE ANNUAL COST TO WASH

Electric water heater

Wash/Rinse cycle	Cost per load at 140°F	Cost per load at 120°F	Annual cost at 140°F	Annual cost at 120°F
Hot/Hot	$.66	$.52	$240.90	$189.80
Hot/Warm	.50	.39	182.50	142.35
Hot/Cold	.34	.27	124.10	98.55
Warm/Warm	.34	.27	124.10	98.55
Warm/Cold	.18	.15	65.70	54.75
Cold/Cold	.03	.03	10.95	10.95

Gas water heater

Wash/Rinse cycle	Cost per load at 140°F	Cost per load at 120°F	Annual cost at 140°F	Annual cost at 120°F
Hot/Hot	$.20	$.15	$73.00	$54.75
Hot/Warm	.15	.10	54.75	36.50
Hot/Cold	.10	.07	36.50	25.55
Warm/Warm	.10	.07	36.50	25.55
Warm/Cold	.05	.04	18.25	14.60
Cold/Cold	.03	.03	10.95	10.95

Electricity, 8 cents per kilowatt hour; gas, 60 cents per therm; annual costs based on 365 loads per year.

eral minutes, then turn the washer on. This saves time, water, and detergent.

To make your clothes last longer, wash clothes with care. Never overload the washing machine; clothes that are stuffed too tightly into the washer tend to rub together and cause pilling. To prevent snags, close all zippers and fasteners before washing.

Before you spend a fortune to dry-clean curtains, check to see if they actually need to be professionally cleaned. The curtains may merely be dusty. If this is the case, toss them in the dryer for a few minutes on air-fluff to get the dust and loose dirt off.

Spray Starch

Make your own inexpensive spray starch.

1 tablespoon cornstarch
2 cups water

Pour into a spray bottle. Shake the mixture before each use. Spray directly on clothing just as you would use a can of aerosol spray starch. If you prefer a heavier starch, use two or three tablespoons of starch.

Speed Dry

Buying a gas clothes dryer usually costs about $50 more than a similar electric model, but you'll quickly start saving money because a gas dryer is much cheaper to operate. The annual cost for a gas dryer is less than half the cost of running an electric model.

To save the most money, dry clothes on a clothesline. When the weather is not suitable for outside drying, hang clothes to dry in the garage or basement. If you have an older electric dryer, you can save up to $75 per year by using a clothesline. Even if you have a late-model gas dryer, you can save $25 per year.

SAVE LOADS ON LAUNDRY COSTS

Throw a dry towel in the dryer with especially damp or bulky clothes. The dry towel will speed up the drying time and save energy.

Do several loads of laundry at a time. When you dry two or more loads in a row, you take advantage of the heat still in the dryer after the first load.

Clean the lint trap in the dryer after each load. A clogged lint filter will restrict airflow, and your dryer will use more energy to get the clothes dry.

Stop the Stains!

To remove "ring around the collar" stains, use inexpensive shampoo, which dissolves body oils. Using a small paintbrush, paint a little shampoo on the stain and let it soak overnight before washing.

Keep plain talcum powder handy. Rub some talcum powder into a spot and let it sit on the spot overnight. A stiff brush will usually remove the entire problem without a costly trip to the cleaners!

ELECTRIC VS. GAS DRYER	Annual Cost to Operate	
Appliance	Pre-1986 Appliance	New
Electric clothes dryer	$75	$59
Gas clothes dryer	30	25
Savings per year	$45	$34

Electricity, 8 cents per kilowatt hour; gas, 60 cents per therm.

SAVE LOADS ON LAUNDRY COSTS

Homemade Stain Remover

You may never have to buy pretreating stain remover again!

- ½ cup ammonia
- ½ cup white vinegar
- ¼ cup baking soda
- 2 tablespoons liquid soap
- 2 quarts water

Mix all ingredients together and pour into a spray bottle. Spray the solution on the stain and let it soak for a few minutes before washing as usual. Shake the solution before each use.

Soap Solutions

Most laundry detergents are highly concentrated. Experiment with the brand that you use. Many times you can use one-half to three-quarters of the recommended amount and get your clothes just as clean. If you have an extra-large-capacity washer or very hard water, you may need to use a little extra detergent to get clothes clean the first time.

If you use a powdered detergent that has a scoop inside, make sure you are not using more than the recommended amount. Some scoops are made to fill all the way to the top, while others have a "fill to" line below the top. Don't use too much detergent. You'll just end up washing the clothes again to get the detergent off.

SAVINGS ON WHEELS

Next to housing, buying a car is the biggest single expense for most people. Not only is the purchase price high, but when you add the cost of repairs, maintenance, gasoline, and insurance, a car is also expensive to operate.

A Little R & R (Research and Reference)

Your first stop, when you go car shopping, should be at the library. There you can find many price reference books and car buying guides. You will be able to find out the dealer's cost on the car you're interested in plus the additional cost for each option added. Once you know the dealer's cost, you will be able to make an offer that is close to cost but high enough for the dealer to accept the offer. If you negotiate hard enough, you should be able to make a deal anywhere from 3 percent to 8 percent over dealer's cost.

You can also find out information on the performance and maintenance records of different models of cars.

The High Cost of Driving

After you have picked out the car you want to buy, you need to consider the annual cost of driving this particular car. You need to consider depreciation, repairs and maintenance costs, gasoline, and the cost of auto insurance.

Depreciation: When you drive a new car off the lot, it immediately starts depreciating. The difference between the estimated resale value and the purchase price is depreciation. If you keep a car four years and drive it 15,000 miles or less per year, the estimated resale value is 38 percent of the original price. Divide the total depreciation by four years to calculate your annual estimated depreciation.

Insurance: Even cars that cost about the same amount of money can have insurance costs that vary hundreds of dollars per year. For a model that has a high theft or accident rate, you'll pay dearly in increased premiums. Before you buy a new car, talk to your insurance agent about how much insurance will cost.

Repairs and maintenance: Estimated maintenance and repair costs should be fairly low, since a new car warranty will cover most major repairs. You'll pay for oil changes and other routine maintenance that is not covered under the warranty.

> *The person who needs a status symbol has no status.*
>
> Anonymous

Gasoline: You can calculate estimated gasoline expenses by dividing your estimated miles per year by the car's estimated mileage per gallon, then multiplying by the current price per gallon of gasoline.

Interest on your auto loan: You can save quite a bit of money by financing for a shorter period of time or making a larger down payment. Of course you can save thousands of dollars by not financing the car, but few of us have $13,000 to $20,000 cash to plunk down for a new car.

Know When to Strike a Deal

A well-informed, patient buyer can get a fair price on a car at almost any time, but it is generally easier to negotiate and get the lowest price when business is slow or the dealer is anxious to liquidate inventory.

SAVINGS ON WHEELS

Best time of the month: The best time to shop for a new car is at the end of the month. At that time, the dealer is not as anxious about covering his overhead costs for the month. On the first day of the new month, the dealer must pay interest on the money he's borrowed for each vehicle on the lot. To avoid having to pay another month of interest, dealers are often motivated to offer a good deal on the 30th or 31st.

There is another reason this end-of-the-month strategy can work. A salesperson may be on a bonus plan and may need only one more sale to make this bonus. The salesperson may be willing to make less commission on your sale in order to meet the required quota.

Best time of day: Go to the dealer at night, an hour or two before closing. The salespeople are tired and ready to go home, but they can't leave as long as a customer is on the property. Another plus for shopping at night: If you are trading in a car, it may not be examined as thoroughly at night—which could get you a higher trade-in allowance.

Best time of the year: Late September or October, when the new models come out and the dealers are eager to move out last year's cars, is the best time of the year to look for a new car. December is also a good month to buy a car, since sales are traditionally slow during the holiday season.

The Trade-in

Consider the option of selling your old car yourself. Place a sign in the window and run a small classified ad in the weekend edition of your local paper. If you don't think selling your car yourself is worth the effort, consider this: The average difference between retail and wholesale selling price, according to the National Auto Dealers Association Used Car Guide, is about $600 to $700. If you plan to sell your car yourself, look up the retail price in the guide and try to sell your car for the retail price. If you plan to trade in your car, look up the wholesale price in the guide. You can expect the dealer to pay you slightly less than the wholesale price.

THE BIGGER, THE BETTER
Often the best car prices are at big volume dealers, because they profit most from manufacturer incentives and they may pass some of the savings on to you. If you have two dealerships close by, get a written estimate from one dealer and see if a competing dealership will beat the quoted price.

Let's Make a Deal
You are expected to deal, bargain, or haggle with the dealer to get the best price. With the exception of a few cars, all dealers will sell cars below the sticker price. If you are not comfortable haggling with a car dealer, the best advice is to hire a haggler. Check with your auto club, credit union, or place of employment to see if they have a car-buying program that gives you prenegotiated prices. Ask a friend or relative who enjoys haggling to go with you and help negotiate the deal. Haggling is a quick way to save several hundred or even over a thousand dollars on your new car.

High Finance, High Cost
Financing a car will cost you thousands of dollars over the life of the loan. To save the most money, you should shop for the lowest interest rate, make a large down payment, and finance the car for a short period

of time. The payment on a 5.5-year loan may look attractive, but you'll end up paying thousands more in interest.

Have the financing lined up before visiting the dealer. Although the dealer will gladly work out the financing for you, you can bet that it won't be the lowest rate in town (unless they are offering a factory-authorized low interest rate). A lower interest rate can save you hundreds of dollars over the life of the loan.

INTERESTING

$13,000 Loan at 8%

Years paid	Payment	Total cost	Interest
3	$407	$14,665	$1,665
4	317	15,234	2,234
5	264	15,815	2,815
5.5	244	16,112	3,112

$13,000 Loan at 9%

Years paid	Payment	Total cost	Interest
3	$413	$14,882	$1,882
4	324	15,528	2,528
5	269	16,132	3,132
5.5	250	16,530	3,530

SAVINGS ON WHEELS

Call several local financial institutions to find the lowest rate. If you are a member of a credit union, don't forget to check its interest rates.

Beware of Add-ons

After you have made the deal, many dealers will start to add costs onto the bill. Typical add-ons are rustproofing and fabric protection. Both of these add-ons are overpriced. Cars are guaranteed by the manufacturers for many years against rust-through. You can get the same fabric protection with a $4 bottle of fabric-guard spray. Some dealerships will also add on a "dealer preparation" charge. This is a last-minute, unexpected add-on. Refuse to pay the dealer preparation charge, and take a pass on the rustproofing and fabric protection.

LEASE VS. PURCHASE	Purchase	Lease
Cost of car	$16,000	$ 0
Monthly payments	398	325
Interest expense	3,104	0
Lease payments	0	15,600
Estimated value (after 4 years)	6,080	0
Net cost	13,024	15,600
Purchase savings	$2,576	

Buying a Used Car

The average car price increases every year, which makes buying a used car more appealing. According to consumer car experts, the best buy in a used car is one that is three years old or less, is in good condition both inside and out, and has been driven no more than 15,000 miles per year. The largest portion of depreciation will already have occurred on the car; any problems or defects will probably have been repaired; and with reasonable care the vehicle should still be reliable for at least another 50,000 miles.

To determine if the car you are looking at is priced fairly, use a guide from the library such as the *Kelley Blue Book*. Guides like this one list the national average sale price, which may or may not apply in your particular area. Compare prices in your local newspaper's classified ads to get a feel for prices in your area.

Look the car over carefully for signs of damage, excessive wear on the upholstery and carpets, missing or broken accessories, repainting, and other signs of trouble. Ask to see the maintenance and repair records. If you are buying from a dealer, ask for the former owner's name and address to check out the maintenance history. Test-drive the car on streets and highways. See how it handles during fast and slow speeds. Listen for unusual noises. Turn on all accessories, including both the heater and air conditioning, to make sure they work.

Finally, if everything looks all right and you are interested in the car, have your mechanic check out the car. To do this, you will have to have the permission of the seller. If the seller refuses to allow your mechanic to inspect it, walk away. The seller must have some reason not to want a mechanic to look at the car.

CHECK THE WARRANTY
If you buy a used car, always check out the warranty situation. Still-valid factory or extended warranties, or even service contracts, can sometimes be transferred to the new owner.

The Lowdown on Leasing

Leasing a car instead of buying it can considerably reduce your up-front money and the amount you pay monthly, but it will cost you more money in the long run. Leasing is more expensive because when you're done paying monthly lease payments on a closed-end lease, you are left with nothing but the need for something to drive. If you buy the car instead of leasing it, you will still have the car when the payments end. The value of the car after four years should far exceed the difference between what you pay for it and what you would pay to lease the car.

Get More Mileage From Your Gasoline

Gasoline will more than likely be your biggest automobile operating expense. Remember that only a few high-performance engines require premium-grade gasoline (91 octane or higher) to avoid pinging. All other cars run on 87 octane, which is 10 cents to 30 cents a gallon cheaper. If you find that one brand knocks, before you spend the extra money on higher octane, keep on trying different brands of gasoline until you find a brand that does not ping. Many people buy high-octane gasoline because they think it will make their car perform better and run faster. This is just not the case.

EASY DISCOUNTS

Two ways to get discounts on gasoline:
1. Pump your own gas. At some stations the price difference between self-service and full service is as much as 20 cents per gallon.
2. Pay cash. You can often save four or five cents per gallon by paying cash instead of charging it.

Don't "top off" your gas tank after the pump automatically shuts off. The gas in your tank will expand when it gets hot, and it can overflow. Spilling gasoline

FOUR WAYS TO SAVE ON AUTO REPAIRS

1. Buy auto supplies such as motor oil and other fluids at a discount auto parts store or a large discount store. You will pay almost double the discount price if you buy these items at the gas station or a convenience store.

2. When you need to replace a part, such as a mirror, glove compartment door, or fender, check out your local salvage yard. This is a good way to save money and recycle.

3. Shop around for routine maintenance services such as oil changes, tune-ups, brakes, and tires. Often a local service station or repair shop will price them much lower than the dealership.

4. Check with your local high school and see if they have an auto mechanic shop class that can do the work. This is a good way to get repair work at a very low price. If you can spare the time, you can save dramatically.

on the concrete and possibly all over yourself is a real waste of money. Pay the $12.48 when the pump shuts off instead of trying to squeeze in 13 bucks' worth!

To get the best gas mileage, empty the junk out of your trunk and check your tire pressure often. A tune-up can significantly increase your gas mileage, too. Call local repair shops and gas stations for a price quote. Prices can vary more than 200 percent!

Make your own car windshield washer fluid by combining one cup of rubbing alcohol, two tablespoons of liquid detergent, and enough water to fill a gallon container. Mix and store the solution in a clean gallon milk container. If desired, add a drop of blue food coloring. The alcohol will prevent the mixture from freezing.

Observe the speed limit. According to the U. S. Department of Energy, the average car uses 17 percent less gasoline at 55 miles per hour than at 65 miles per hour.

Compare Auto Clubs

Before you sign up or renew your auto club membership, think about the services you will use and how much membership costs. Most people join an auto club for the towing benefit. If you fall into this category, check with your auto insurance about towing coverage. In states that allow this type of coverage, the costs are minimal, usually about $10 to $20 per year.

Lower Your Auto Insurance

If you have more than one car, you may be able to save 15 to 20 percent on auto insurance by insuring all of them with the same insurance company on the same policy.

Comparison shop your auto insurance each year. Rates can change drastically from year to year. When your driving record or situation changes, another company may offer a better rate than your current insurance company's. Some companies will raise your rates through the roof when you get a speeding ticket; others may be more lenient. When you add a driver, such as an inexperienced teenager, expect rates to vary quite a bit from one company to another.

Always ask about discounts. Discounts may be offered for being a good student, for taking a driver training course, or for driving fewer than a stipulated number of miles each year. Other discounts may be available for senior citizens; for cars with automatic seat belts, air bags, or anti-theft devices; or even for women who are the only driver in a household.

Increase the deductible on your auto policy and bank the savings. Increasing your deductible from $200 to $500 could reduce your collision premium by 15 to 35 percent. Put the premium savings into a bank account; then if you have to make a claim, you won't have a hard time scraping up the deductible.

If you have an older car, consider dropping your collision and comprehensive coverage. If your car is worth less than $2,500, you'll quickly pay out more in premiums than you would be able to collect.

CLOTHING ON THE CHEAP

No one magic formula can get you the best clothing bargains every time. Sometimes you can find bargains at the most unlikely places. Knowing when and where to look for the best buys can get you top-notch clothing for bargain-basement prices.

Specialty Shops

Specialty shops usually limit their inventory to one type of merchandise, such as lingerie, handbags and accessories, children's clothing, sportswear, and so on. You can expect the regular prices to be higher at specialty shops. But you can also find some really terrific bargains when they clear out merchandise two or three times a year. If you like the merchandise, but the prices are high, ask when they will take the final markdowns. Many of these stores have a set schedule for marking down merchandise, and the final markdown may be 75 to 80 percent off.

Department Stores

Department stores offer a large selection of clothing. They typically carry a wide range of quality and prices. Frequently the better, more upscale department stores will surprise you with prices that are comparable to or even lower than those offered by discount or chain stores. Look for end-of-season sales at the best department stores. They like to liquidate end-of-season merchandise quickly, so they drastically mark down clothing to move it out of the store.

Discount and Chain Stores

Prices in discount and chain stores tend to be lower than the prices in department stores, but the quality of clothing also tends to be lower. Frequent problems are poor construction (pull a string and the whole garment falls apart) or fading (wash the item three or four times and it looks worn out). Generally, the best buys at discount and chain stores are socks, underwear, pajamas, sweatshirts and sweatpants, and jeans (look for a name brand).

Factory Outlets

Years ago factory outlets sold just overstocks, overruns, display goods, samples, seconds, and irregulars, and most items were bargain-priced. Today factory outlets still exist and they do carry some discontinued merchandise, overstocks, and flawed merchandise, but they supplement the inventory with first-quality new clothing at retail prices. The best buys at a factory outlet generally are seconds and marked-down merchandise. First-quality merchandise at a factory outlet store may or may not be cheaper than the exact same item at a department store.

Don't buy into those price tags that show an inflated retail price. Keep in mind that no one actually paid the retail price shown for the item. Also keep in mind that you may be able to find the same item at a department store for less. Always comparison shop for the lowest prices.

Secondhand Clothing

You can find some incredible bargains on used clothing. One woman bought her beautiful wedding gown for $5, and another found a tailor-made tuxedo for her husband for $35. The selection will be limited, but the prices will be low.

There are several ways to get secondhand clothing. The cheapest way to get it is in the form of hand-me-downs from another family member, a friend, or a relative. You can also find used clothing at yard sales, church bazaars, flea markets, consignment shops, and thrift stores.

When shopping for used clothing, look for well-made clothing. Instead of shopping for a specific item, such as a blue blazer with gold buttons, look at what they have in your size and try to find pieces that will

---

LABEL LINGO

Confused about the different types of merchandise for sale at factory outlet stores? Clothing experts say that about 80 percent of outlet merchandise is first-quality, but some of the best buys are slightly flawed. Here's what the labels mean.

Irregular: These items will have tiny imperfections but no serious flaws. If you wear irregular pantyhose, for example, no one will be able to notice any imperfections.

Seconds: This is flawed merchandise. Usually the merchandise is wearable, but you need to carefully inspect it to make sure it meets your needs.

Samples: These items have been on display and may appear shopworn. The colors may not exactly match coordinating pieces. Sizes and colors will be limited.

Past season: Last year's styles are this year's best buys. As long as the style is still being worn, past-season merchandise can be some of the best bargains.

Discontinued: These items are no longer manufactured, so stores are getting rid of the last pieces. Sizes and colors will usually be limited.

go with clothing you already own. Examine the clothing carefully before buying. If it has a noticeable stain, assume that you will not be able to get it out. On the other hand, if it needs just a little repair work, such as mending a hole along the seam, you probably can fix that problem quickly.

Consignment Shops

A consignment shop carries used clothing and pays the owner of the clothing if the item is sold. Most consignment shops carry women's or children's clothing.

A few stores also have a limited selection of men's clothing. Consignment shops generally carry high-quality, barely worn clothing. The styles will be up-to-date or classic fashions that never go out of style. Articles that are accepted for consignment must be almost new-looking. You can find good-looking clothing at a fraction of what it would cost new. Consignment shops will have a dressing room so that you can

The chief ingredient that makes expensive merchandise so expensive is profit.

Anonymous

try clothing on before buying. Some of the best buys in consignment shops are special-occasion clothing, such as formal dresses for proms, weddings, or parties, and business wear such as jackets and suits.

Consignment shops are also an easy way to make some extra money when you clean out your closet. Simply take your clothing, clean and on hangers, to the consignment shop owner or manager. The shop owner may accept new items only at a certain time or on a certain day of the week, so it is best to ask before dropping off clothing. The shop owner or manager will set the price and generally, if the item sells, the sales price is split fifty-fifty. Consigning clothing truly is a win-win-win situation. The shop owner wins by making a commission on the clothes sold. The consignee wins by making some money from clothing that would end up being discarded, donated, or sold at a garage sale for a lower price. And the shopper wins by getting quality used clothing at a low price.

Shop thrift stores and consignment shops near upscale neighborhoods. You'll find the best merchandise, since people with higher incomes tend to buy high-quality clothes and replace them often.

Thrift Stores

Thrift stores may carry a wide assortment of merchandise, but you can bet that much of the store will be filled with clothing. Thrift stores are sponsored by the Salvation Army, Goodwill, American Veterans, and other charitable or nonprofit organizations. The items they sell are collected through donations. The quality of merchandise will vary tremendously. You can find items that look like new at bargain prices. A thrift store may or may not have a dressing room. Some thrift stores offer discounts to seniors, and some run special mark-down sales from time to time.

Q. Does a designer label indicate better-quality clothing?

A. For the most part, no. A few very high-priced designer clothing lines are of exceptional quality. But in most cases the designer has simply allowed his or her name to be placed on the garments. Typically a designer or celebrity will sell the rights to their name to a clothing manufacturer. The manufacturer then pays the designer or celebrity a certain amount of money for each piece of clothing sold. The clothing may not even be unique. Some manufacturers put different labels on identical articles of clothing. The only difference will be the price, and that difference can be many dollars.

Quality Assurance

Well-made clothing will last through many seasons of wear. If you buy cheap clothing that is poorly constructed, you will pay more for it in the long run. Here's what to look for when buying new or used clothes to get the most for your money:

Look at the stitching. Small, close stitching usually means a garment will hold up to washing and wearing. Stitches should be neat, straight, and even. Lots of strings hanging down from the garment indicate poor workmanship.

Look for gathers or puckering at the seams or darts. All seams should be flat; even a slight puckering at the seams should be avoided.

Look for evenly woven fabric with no flaws. Some natural fibers have small flaws that do not detract from the garment. Other flaws, especially in artificial fibers, should be avoided.

Plaids, stripes, and checks should match at the seams. Armhole and crotch cross seams should match up. If they do not match, it is a sure sign of poor quality.

Pockets should be flat, with reinforced corners, and they should be large enough to use comfortably.

Snaps, buttons, buckles, and other trim items should be neatly secured with enough thread to keep them from falling off.

Zippers should be sewn in straight, should lie flat, and should be dyed to match the fabric of the garment.

Buttonholes should be reinforced. Ones that are sewn through both sides of the fabric hold up especially well.

Hems should be straight, and hem stitches should be invisible on the outside of the garment.

Label Lookout

Always read the label when buying clothes, and be on the lookout for dry-clean-only tags. Business clothing such as blazers or suits will have to be sent to the dry cleaners, but to save money, stay away from casual clothing that must be dry-cleaned. Even if the price of the garment is right, the price of dry cleaning will make the garment expensive. You'll quickly spend more money on dry cleaning than you paid for the clothing.

How to Save on Dry Cleaning

If the little words "dry-clean only" make you want to scream, here are some tips to keep the high cost of dry cleaning under control.

Wash delicate clothes by hand or use the gentle cycle of the washing machine. Chances are that many of the shirts, blouses, and dresses that you're dry-cleaning are hand-washable. Garments of cotton, nylon, silk, ramie, and polyester can be washed by hand as long as they are colorfast. To test for color-fastness, blot a white rag dipped in hot water on an inside, unexposed seam of the garment. If the color comes off onto the white rag, you'll have to have the garment dry-cleaned. Some materials such as acetate and viscose rayon will shrink substantially if laundered, so they need to be dry-cleaned.

Dry-clean less frequently. After each wearing, remove soil from jackets or coats by brushing with a soft-bristled brush. Let wrinkles smooth out by allowing them to hang for a few days. Many times a skirt or pair of suit pants just needs to have the wrinkles ironed out.

Always dry-clean the entire suit. Don't be tempted to have just the pants or skirt cleaned and wait until next time to clean the jacket. Dry cleaning can slightly change the color of your garments, so over time the two parts of your suit may not be the same color.

Point out any stains and let your cleaner know exactly what the stain is. Dry cleaners are very proficient at removing stains. If the stain is not treated when the garment is cleaned, however, the stain will be harder to remove and may be permanent.

Buy clothes from the dry cleaner. Once a year many dry cleaners will sell off the clothes that have not been picked up. Most will sell them for the price of the cleaning!

Saving on Pantyhose

Many women spend a staggering amount of money each year on pantyhose. You can cut costs dramatically by ordering pantyhose through the mail. See page 51 for the information.

Buy several pairs of the same brand and color of pantyhose. When you get a run in one pair, cut off the bad leg just below the panty. When a matching pair gets a run in the other leg, you can wear the two panty tops, each with its one good leg.

If the Shoe Fits, Wear It

Since shoes can be among the most expensive items in your closet, it makes sense to buy shoes that fit well and are made to last. Here are some tips on getting the best fit.

Try on shoes late in the day when your feet are swollen. Wear the same type of hosiery or socks that you plan to wear with the shoes. The thickness of socks can make a big difference in fit.

Always try on both shoes of the pair. Walk around for a few minutes to make sure they feel comfortable. If they aren't comfortable in the store, don't buy them. Don't count on the shoes being comfortable after they're broken in.

A good fit is more important than the size of the shoes. Sizing varies from one manufacturer to another. Even different styles by the same manufacturer may fit differently, so time spent trying on shoes is not a waste of time.

Shoes should be wide enough for you to comfortably wiggle your toes. The front of the shoe should not pinch or squeeze toes. The back of the shoe should be tight enough to grip your heel and not slip when you walk.

Look for classic styles of shoes that never go out of style, such as pumps, loafers, dock-siders, and wing tips. With proper care, you'll be able to wear them for years.

The Shoe Doctor

You'll save money by replacing soles and heels on your old dress shoes instead of buying a new pair of shoes. While you're at the shoe repair shop, ask what preventative steps you can take to keep your shoes from wearing down.

CLOTHING ON THE CHEAP

When shoelace ends get frayed and hard to lace, try this: Twist the ends tightly (you may have to dampen them a bit). Dip them into clear nail polish and let dry.

RUNS AND SNAGS

Want to make your pantyhose last longer? Try these tips.

Add a drop or two of fabric softener to the final rinse. It lubricates the fibers and adds life to your hose.

Buy pantyhose with reinforced toes. They are less vulnerable to snags and holes in the toe area.

Buy the largest size that will fit properly. The less stress on the fabric, the longer the pantyhose will last.

Put new pantyhose in the freezer overnight before wearing them. Although some clothing experts think this is just an old wives' tale, others believe freezing pantyhose seems to make the fibers resist running.

Support pantyhose will save you money in the long run, even though they cost more to buy. The fabric is much more durable and will stand up to more washings and everyday wear.

Remove jewelry and make sure your hands are smooth before you put your pantyhose on. Rings and long fingernails can snag or run pantyhose. Apply lotion if necessary to smooth your hands.

Once a month or so, soak pantyhose in salt water before washing. Salt will coat the fibers and make them stronger. Add about half a cup of salt for each quart of water. Soak pantyhose for a half hour or longer, then wash as usual.

Your laces will be like new again. To keep the tips on new shoelaces from breaking off, dip them in clear nail polish and let dry before you wear them.

In the car, you get scraped heels and ugly scuff marks on your shoes while driving. To keep your shoes looking new longer, keep a pair of old slip-ons in the car to change into.

To keep canvas tennis shoes new-looking longer, spray them with a light coating of starch before wearing them the first time. You can use the recipe on page 24. The starch will help the shoes stay clean longer. After washing your tennis shoes, apply another coat of spray starch to them as soon as they are dry. If you apply spray starch to your shoes after each washing, you will find that you do not need to wash them as often, which will make them last longer.

> I would rather have my people laugh at my economies than weep for my extravagance.
>
> Anonymous

When you buy a new pair of tennis shoes, don't automatically throw away the old ones. Save them to wear around the house and while working in the yard. This will help your new shoes stay new-looking longer. Keep the oldest pair of shoes in the garage for mowing the lawn or doing any especially dirty yard work.

To increase the life of your workout shoes, wear them only for exercise. If your workout shoes get wet, stuff them with rolled-up newspapers to help absorb the moisture. When shoes are left wet, they lose their shape, and the moisture speeds up the breakdown of shoe materials.

Here's an easy way to dry out wet tennis shoes. Place the shoes on the floor in front of the refrigerator by the grille overnight. The movement from the fan inside will thoroughly dry out the shoes. Shoes dried this way will keep their shape better than shoes dried in the clothes dryer. This method is quieter and requires no extra electricity.

Frugal Formal Wear

When you get invited to a formal event, it's not necessary to break your budget to outfit yourself. There are several ways to look terrific without spending big bucks.

If you are lucky enough to have a close friend or relative who wears the same dress size, you can borrow formal dresses and accessories from each other.

Consignment shops and thrift stores almost always have a large selection of formal dresses. Shop early for holiday or prom dresses, because the best dresses will fly off the racks when the occasion gets near.

Rent a dress instead of buying it. You can rent a very expensive dress or gown for much less than the cost of buying one. Look in the yellow pages under "formal wear" to find stores that rent women's formal gowns and dresses.

It is cheaper for a man who attends formal events to buy a basic black tuxedo instead of renting one every time. Even if you attend just one or two formal events per year, a tuxedo will quickly pay for itself. Consignment shops frequently have men's tuxedos for less than the price of one rental. You can buy used tuxedo shoes, shirts, bow ties, and cummerbunds from a tuxedo rental shop for less than half the original cost.

IT'S IN THE MAIL

Here is a short list of some of the best mail-order bargains.

Checks on the Cheap

You do not have to order checks through the bank where you have your checking account. Checks from your local bank can cost as much as $15 for 200 checks. Mail-order check companies can cost about half as much. These companies have a large selection of check styles; you should find a style you like. Most companies offer a low introductory price for the first order. Call one of the companies listed to get a catalog and more information.

Current
1-800-533-3973
Artistic Checks
1-800-224-7621
Checks in the Mail
1-800-733-4443

Current also sells low-cost greeting cards and accessories.

Magazine Subscriptions

These companies offer low-cost magazine subscriptions. No sweepstakes, no gimmicks, just the absolute lowest prices. Split the cost of subscribing to magazines with a friend, and you'll save even more! Call for a catalog.

Delta Publishing Group
1-800-728-3728
Below Wholesale Magazines
1-800-800-0063

AARP Pharmacy

The American Association of Retired Persons has a discount mail-order pharmacy that anyone, regardless of age, can use. It is a complete, full-line drugstore that carries both prescription medication and over-the-counter items. Their prices are hard to beat! Call for a quote.

AARP Pharmacy
1-800-456-2226

Computer Deals

Low-cost computer supplies and software are offered by mail-order. Delivery charges for most items are just $3 for overnight delivery! Their prices are generally lower than discount computer superstores. Call for a catalog.

Mac Warehouse
1-800-255-6227
Tiger Software
1-800-888-4437

A Leg Up on Savings

Showcase of Savings sells pantyhose, lingerie, socks, T-shirts, nightclothes, and other such items at drastically reduced prices. The pantyhose are imperfect or "seconds," but don't worry; you won't be able to find the flaws. Satisfaction is guaranteed. Call for a catalog.

Showcase of Savings
1-800-522-9567

For the Home

Domestications' catalog offers low-cost sheets, blankets, comforters, curtains, rugs, and other accessories for the home. These items make low-cost decorating easy. Call for a catalog.

Domestications
1-800-746-2555

Couch Potato Shopping

It may be hard to resist ordering merchandise sold on television. The hosts can make everything look so beautiful and sound like such a bargain. Keep in mind that very few real bargains are offered on television shopping networks. Make sure you understand the return policy before buying anything offered on a shopping network or infomercial. They may allow you to return the item, but you will probably pay the postage and handling both ways, which could cost more than the actual product. Buyer beware!

The Golden Age of Savings

Age has its privileges. If you are 50 years old or older you can qualify for all sorts of senior citizen discounts. The best advice for seniors is to speak up and ask! Senior discounts may—or may not—be listed or posted. Every time you spend money, ask if a discount is available. You'll be surprised at the places that offer a discount. Some stores offer seniors a discount on a special day of the week, generally Tuesday or Wednesday. Find out when your favorite stores offer discounts and do most of your shopping then. Here are just a few of the many special offers available only to seniors.

AARP membership. The American Association of Retired Persons is a nonprofit organization open to anyone over the age of 50. You don't have to be actually retired to join. The membership is very inexpensive—just $8 for one year, $20 for three years, or

$45 for ten years. The membership fee also includes your spouse. With an AARP membership, you get such benefits as discounts on hotels, motels, car rentals, and resorts. The AARP mails out a monthly bulletin and a bimonthly magazine. For more information, call 202-434-AARP.

Banking. Most banks offer special rates, freebies, and incentives to seniors. You should be able to find no-fee checking accounts, discounted or free safe deposit box rental, and free traveler's checks. Special offers for seniors will vary from one bank to another, so shop around to find the best bargains on services you regularly use.

Discount greens fees. If you are over 65, you can get reduced greens fees at most public and many private golf courses. Have your proof of age with you and always ask about the discount before paying.

Golden Age Passport. You must be at least 62 years old to buy this lifetime pass. It will admit you free of charge to any federal park, monument, forest, or recreation area that charges an admittance fee. The cost is just $10, and with the pass, anyone in your noncommercial vehicle also gets in free. You can pick up the pass at any national park where entrance fees are charged. For more information, write:

National Park Service
P. O. Box 37127
Washington, DC 20013

BEAUTY ON A BUDGET

You can spend a small fortune on beauty products, and many of them don't work any better than a much cheaper alternative. Makeup remover, for instance—why pay an inflated price for a fancy brand when baby oil or even plain mineral oil works just as well? Baby oil and mineral oil won't irritate the eyes, and they also act as natural moisturizers.

A high price doesn't always indicate a better product; it usually indicates higher advertising costs. When buying beauty aids, read the label and ingredients. You'll be surprised at how similar some products really are. You don't have to pay the high price when a low-cost or generic alternative is available.

COSMETICS ON THE CHEAP

Cosmetics	Low-cost substitutes
Makeup remover	Baby oil, mineral oil
Perfume	Cologne
Bath oil	Baby oil, vegetable oil
Deodorant	Baking soda
Cold cream	Vegetable shortening
Dusting powder	Baby powder, cornstarch
Toothpaste	Baking soda
Denture cleanser	Vinegar

NATIONAL BRAND VS. GENERIC BRAND	Generic brand	National brand	Savings	Percent saved
Baby oil (20 ounces)	$.99	$2.79	$1.80	65%
Mouthwash (32 ounces)	1.48	3.29	1.81	55%
Petroleum jelly (16 ounces)	1.29	3.89	2.60	67%
Deodorant (1.75 ounces)	.99	1.89	.90	48%

Prices are from a single week in 1995.

Where you purchase your health and beauty aids can make a big difference in the cost. Picking them up at the grocery store may be convenient, but you'll wind up paying a much higher price for them. Find a discount drugstore in your area that offers deep discounts on health and beauty aids. Their prices make it worth an extra trip once or twice a month to stock up on toiletries.

Lipstick for Less

You can pay up to $20 for a tube of lipstick at the cosmetics counters in a department store. Have you ever wondered what makes these tubes cost so much more than the brands available at the drugstore? According to one report, all lipsticks are pretty much the same. The basic ingredients—wax, oil, dye, and perfume—are the same whether you spend $2 for a tube or $20.

What the high-priced lipsticks usually offer you is a better case, more fragrance, and a classier image. The performance is about the same. So before you spend $20 on a tube of designer lipstick, shop the discount drugstore to see what's available. For the same amount of money, you can get enough different colors to match every outfit and mood.

Makeup Mistakes

When buying makeup, use a tester or sample first, if at all possible. Remember, what looks great in the store might look horrible in natural sunlight. If you are not careful, you could end up with a whole drawer of makeup mistakes, and this adds up to major dollars.

SAVE AT THE DISCOUNT STORE

	Discount store	Grocery store	Savings	Percent saved
Shampoo (11 ounces)	$.89	$1.99	$1.10	55%
Toothpaste (8.2 ounces)	1.75	2.79	1.04	37%
Shaving cream (11 ounces)	.79	1.39	.60	43%
Mouthwash (33.8 ounces)	3.29	4.99	1.70	34%

Prices are for products of the same brand from a single week in 1995.

Always save your receipt when you try a new type or color of makeup. If you are not satisfied with the makeup, don't just toss it in a drawer. Return it to the store where you purchased it. Most stores will either give you a cash refund or a store credit. If the store will not refund your money, call or write to the company that makes the product. Explain the problem and ask for a refund. Most companies will bend over backward to make sure you are satisfied.

Rub-a-Dub-Dub, Savings for the Tub

Instead of buying a pricey bottle of bath oil, make your own. Buy a low-cost generic or store-brand bottle of baby oil, add a few drops of your favorite perfume, and shake to mix. If you want it to look pretty, add a few drops of food coloring. Add about a tablespoon to your bathwater for a luxurious bath.

> That man is the richest, whose pleasures are the cheapest.
>
> Henry David Thoreau (1817-1862)

For a refreshing bath, add a half cup of baking soda to your bathwater. It makes a refreshing bath additive that costs just a few pennies. A baking soda bath is great for sore muscles and fatigue.

To make your own bubble bath, combine two cups of vegetable oil, three tablespoons of liquid shampoo, and a few drops of your favorite perfume. Mix the solution with a whisk or put it in the blender for a few seconds. Pour into a plastic bottle. Add one or two tablespoons to the bathwater. This formula will make your skin soft and save you money to boot!

Frugal Skin Solutions

Make your own facial cleansing grains by mixing a teaspoon of sugar with your soap lather. This mixture will help remove any dead skin cells. Your skin will feel very soft after using this solution.

To dry up a blemish or pimple, dab the area with lemon juice several times a day. Lemon juice works just as well as any of the expensive products available for a fraction of the cost. Or make a paste of baking soda and peroxide and apply before going to bed.

Homemade Facial Mask

This mask cleans and revitalizes your skin for just a few pennies.

  1 tablespoon instant dry milk
  ½ cucumber, peeled
  1 teaspoon plain yogurt

Puree the ingredients in a blender until smooth. Apply the mixture to your face, avoiding the eye area. Let it dry for about 20 minutes. Rinse off with cool water and pat skin dry. To save time you can make several batches at once. Freeze the extra mixture in an ice cube tray; thaw out as needed.

Savings Can Be Beautiful

To get every last bit of lotion out of a bottle, put it in the microwave for 15 to 20 seconds to get it warm (not hot). Or toss the bottle in your bathwater to warm it up; the warm lotion will pour right out of the bottle.

Refill trial size bottles of lotion, shampoo, and other toiletries for traveling. When you return from your vacation, save the bottles for your next trip. Buying travel sizes each time you take a trip will quickly add

BEAUTY ON A BUDGET

up, but you can refill them yourself for just a couple of pennies.

To make your disposable razor last longer, store it in the medicine cabinet instead of the shower. Moisture in the shower will cause the blade to rust.

Q. I remember my aunt making a face cleanser out of mayonnaise and some other ingredients. What is a recipe for an inexpensive face cleanser?

A. Here's a homemade recipe. Mix $1/2$ cup of mayonnaise with 1 tablespoon melted butter and the juice of one lemon. Place the face cream in a glass jar and store in the refrigerator. Just take a little out and use it to clean your face and remove any makeup. This will clean and soften your skin. Rinse your face with cold water after cleaning with this homemade formula. One batch will last for a long time.

Hair Care

Want to save some cash on haircuts? Check with local beauty schools and see when class is in session. At many schools you can get your hair cut free of charge during the class. Either the instructor will cut it as a demonstration to the class, or a student will cut it with close supervision by the instructor. Even if the cosmetology school does not offer a haircut as a class demonstration, it will probably offer haircuts and other services for 50 to 60 percent less than a beauty salon. Ask about other services such as coloring or permanent waves. You are not usually required to make an appointment, so you can get your hair cut when it's convenient for you.

To save money when coloring your hair, pick a hair color close to your natural color (a shade or two lighter or darker). With a close shade, you won't have to touch up the color as often. When buying hair color, look for a beauty supply store; the price will be much cheaper than buying it at the drugstore (usually about half price).

Want to save on haircuts for the kids? Try cutting their hair yourself. The current short hairstyles for boys are especially easy to cut. Check out a book or video from the library on haircutting and learn to cut your kids' hair. You'll have to buy a few tools, but you can save quite a bit of money over the course of a year. Even if you don't feel confident doing a complete haircut, you can trim the bangs out of your kids' eyes to extend the time between haircuts.

When you think your shampoo bottle is empty, fill it one-third full with water. You'll be amazed at how many more shampoos you'll get!

Skinflint Smile

To get all the toothpaste out of the tube, slip a barrette or an old-fashioned clothespin on the tube. Either one works just as well as the plastic keys that you can buy, and you probably have one or the other lying around the house. When you think the tube of toothpaste is empty, place the closed tube under warm water for a few minutes to get every last drop out of the tube. Then cut open the tube—there's enough for several more brushings.

Homemade Toothpaste

   1 tablespoon baking soda
   ½ teaspoon salt
   ¼ teaspoon peppermint extract

Mix all ingredients together in a small bowl and use as toothpaste. It works great and even tastes great!

Nail it!

Before applying nail polish, rub your fingernails with cotton balls dipped in vinegar. This not only cleans your nails thoroughly, it also will help nail polish stay on longer. Making your polish stay on longer will save you money and valuable time.

Don't throw away nail polish that is too thick to use. Place the old bottle in a pan of hot water for a few minutes to thin it out and restore its smooth consistency.

You don't have to spend extra money on a special quick-drying topcoat or spray to dry nail polish quickly. Instead simply dip your painted nails into ice-cold water to harden your manicure in a hurry.

Sweet Smell of Perfume

To make your cologne or perfume fragrance last longer, dab a little petroleum jelly on your wrists and mix your perfume or cologne with it. The petroleum jelly will make the fragrance last about twice as long. You can put perfume on less often and still enjoy the fragrance all day long.

Shop for perfume bargains after Christmas. Look for special holiday packages of your favorite fragrance. Stock up and save at least 50 percent.

WINTER

Though winter can be the most expensive season of all, you can find ways to have a festive and fun holiday season without spending a bundle. With low-cost gift ideas, party tips, and cheap wrapping suggestions, you'll have fun during the holidays, but the costs won't creep up on you. You can also take steps to reduce the expense of heating your home. Furthermore, you can start off the new year with a new savings plan that will get you a nice nest egg by the end of the year.

SUPERMARKET STRATEGIES

Grocery stores come in all sizes and types—convenience stores, box stores, superstores, discount
stores, warehouse stores, and thrift stores. You can
find some bargains at each type of store if you know
what to look for.

Supermarkets: Supermarkets are full-service grocery stores. They are usually owned by a large corporation that buys in such high volume that significant
price breaks can be passed on to shoppers. Supermarkets also carry a "house brand" of merchandise that is
usually priced lower than the nationally advertised
brands. Most supermarkets have a weekly flyer of advertised specials. Each week one or more items advertised in the flyer will be priced low enough to encourage consumers to do their weekly shopping at the
store.

Superstores: Similar to supermarkets, superstores
are much bigger and have many more departments.
Some of the newest superstores have a full-size discount drug store (with a full-size grocery store under
the same roof). They also may have a branch bank, a
fast-food restaurant, and many other special services
inside. These stores are almost like a minimall. So
much territory to cover can make a superstore hard to
shop. You'll find low prices on most food items and
discounted drug items. You'll find higher prices in special departments such as a gourmet shop or an im-
ported wine and cheese shop.

Convenience stores: Local convenience stores are
not for the frugal-minded; for the most part, their
prices are extremely high. They offer convenience and
long hours—many are open 24 hours a day—instead
of low prices. A convenience store at a filling station

may offer low prices on gasoline, hoping you'll pick up a few impulse items while you're inside the store.

THE $100 CLUB

You can easily call a discount membership warehouse store the $100 club, because it's hard to get out without spending $100. One of the great dangers of warehouse shopping is that you assume everything is cheaper and go on a shopping spree!

If you have a small family, warehouse shopping probably will not save you money. And if you shop with coupons, keep in mind that most discount membership warehouses do not accept any coupons. But if you can use larger quantities and have room to store the extra goodies, you can find some bargains at the warehouse club.

Don't assume you're getting the lowest price just because you're buying it from a warehouse club. Always compare prices to your regular grocery store's—and don't forget to factor in the warehouse club membership fee. Some prices are in fact lower at the warehouse club if you are able to use the large quantities the products come in. Condiments such as ketchup and mustard are bargains, but once you open the large cans, you need smaller containers and space in your refrigerator. Many times you can find the same items at the supermarket for the same price or even less, especially during a sale. The good news is that at the supermarket you don't have to buy three boxes to get the low price.

Beware of the tendency to overbuy at warehouse clubs. Go in with a list and stick to it.

Other convenience stores may offer one or two low prices per week on items such as beer, soft drinks, or milk.

Before you spend the money on a membership to a warehouse club, ask for a one-day free pass to shop and compare prices. Check to see if you are eligible for a free membership through your work or some other organization such as a credit union. At some clubs, by the time you pay the annual fee and an additional 5 percent above the posted prices, you are not getting a bargain!

Box stores: Box stores offer a no-frills shopping experience, although most box stores will accept personal checks and coupons. The merchandise is usually very limited. You'll have few choices of brands and sizes, but the prices are low. You may be able to find the lowest prices overall in a box store. If you don't mind bagging your own groceries and your family is not too picky about brands, you can save quite a bit each week by shopping at a box store.

Thrift stores: Thrift stores are frequently called day-old bread stores. The merchandise is usually limited to a single manufacturer's bakery items such as bread, buns, sweet rolls, cookies, cakes, muffins, and doughnuts. You can save about 40 percent on these items. If you have a large family (or a teenager or two) that quickly eats everything you buy, a thrift store can really stretch your food budget. Most thrift stores will accept personal checks, but they will not accept coupons. The manufacturer expects you to use the coupons for full-priced merchandise.

SUPERMARKET STRATEGIES

Stop Impulse Spending!

It pays to plan ahead when grocery shopping. Without a list and at least a general menu plan, you'll spend more money at the store. Use these strategies to stop impulse buying. Keep a list on the refrigerator and write down items as they are used up. Train your family members to add to the list if they use the last of something.

Take an inventory before going to the store. Check the pantry, refrigerator, and freezer for staples. Add any items you're low on to your list.

Make a master list of items that you regularly buy. Quickly go down the list, check off the needed items, and add any other items to the bottom of the list.

Make a weekly menu and review recipes to include any needed items on the list.

Review advertised specials in the supermarket ad supplements to the newspaper. Plan your menus around the low prices to save.

Fast-Food Savings

Make it a habit to keep your pantry and freezer filled with basic items for a quick, easy meal. If you have something you can get on the table in a hurry, you reduce your chances of going out to eat. Even one unplanned fast-food dinner can put your food budget in the red.

Let It Rain!

Lower your grocery bill by taking advantage of rain checks. Stores frequently run door-buster sales that draw such a huge response that they sell out of the item before the end of the sale. Stop in the store near the end of the sale and see if they are indeed out of the item; if so, ask at the service desk for a rain check. Most stores have liberal policies for cashing in rain checks—some will give you up to a year to use a rain check. So buy the limit on the tuna fish when it is advertised for 49 cents a can. Then check back later in the week. If they still have the tuna, buy more at the low price. If not, get a rain check and buy it whenever you need it at the door-buster price.

Once Is Enough

How many times have you run to the store "just for milk" and wound up spending $50 or more? Limit your grocery shopping trips to once a week or even once every two weeks. If you must go to the store for just an item or two, don't walk down all the aisles to see if you can find something else you need.

Go It Alone

Leave your children at home, and don't take your spouse with you when grocery shopping unless he or she is a thrifty shopper. Children and spouses often encourage extra spending.

Eat Before You Shop

You've probably heard it before, but it's worth saying again: Don't grocery shop when you are hungry. You'll spend more money on junk food than you normally would. Everything looks good, especially the high-priced snacks and convenience foods that are ready to eat. Eat an apple or a peanut butter sandwich before shopping if you are hungry.

Kick the Habit

Avoid buying by habit. Always look for new or different alternatives that may be cheaper and better. Most people tend to buy the same items each week. Continue to comparison shop, and bear in mind that even products that were once the least expensive may become high-priced when compared to other brands and sizes.

It Pays to Weigh

In the produce department, look for the best buys on produce that is in season. In-season produce should be at the peak of freshness and at the lowest price of the year. Always weigh any produce that is sold in a five-pound, ten-pound, or 20-pound bag. You will be surprised at the weight difference between two bags of fruit or vegetables supposedly of equal weight. Look for a bag that seems to be a little fuller than the others. Also, weigh produce sold by the piece rather than by the pound and buy the heavier pieces to get the most for your money.

Buys from the Butcher

Don't be fooled by large "family packs" of pork chops and chicken pieces. Sometimes the meat is the same price per pound as the meat in the smaller packages. Don't buy a package of four pieces of meat when you know your family will eat only three pieces. Ring for the butcher and ask that the package be split up. Most meat departments will repackage items for you at no additional cost.

The service you get from the butcher will vary from store to store. Check out local meat markets, too; you may be able to buy better-quality meats, packaged to order, at a cheaper price per pound from a local meat market. Look for a busy meat market with the volume of customers that can result in better prices and fresher meat.

Sweet Deal

Stay away from anything presweetened, such as instant tea, cereal, and packaged soft drinks. Why pay four or five times more for a product with sugar? Add your own sugar at home.

High-Priced Packaging

Don't pay extra for fancy packaging. You may actually be paying more for the package than the contents! Individual serving packages of juices or puddings cost double or triple the price per ounce of larger packages because of the extra packaging. In the produce department, look for loose vegetables instead of prepackaged ones. You can buy just enough for your family, and you save by not paying for the packaging.

Quality Store Brands

Don't be afraid to try store brands or generics. Most are high-quality products. Start with the product that

GENUINE GENERICS

You can't lose on these generic products, since they have the same chemical makeup no matter whose label is on it. Why pay extra for a name brand?

Baking soda	Molasses
Cooking oils (except olive oil)	Orange juice
Cornstarch	Salt
Extracts (flavorings)	Sugar
Honey	Unbleached flour
Lemon or lime juice	White vinegar

> *Economy is a strange thing: it means buying the big size in a box of cereal, and the small size in a car.*
>
> *Anonymous*

is least expensive per ounce, and work your way up if the quality is not up to your standards. The store brands and even some generic brands are often the same products, supplied by the same companies that make the national brands, with different labels and at much lower prices. The advertising budgets of the national brands increase the prices of the products.

Down with Downsizing

Watch container and package sizes closely. Manufacturers change products all the time. A can of tomatoes may contain 16 ounces one week and 15 ounces the next. The price will be the same—or maybe even more—and it will usually look exactly like the old can, so most people will not even notice that they are getting less for their money. Always compare prices per ounce!

Is Bigger Better?

Bigger is not always better or cheaper. Large "economy" sizes are often the best buy, but don't assume they are always the cheapest per ounce or serving. Sometimes buying two small boxes or bags is cheaper than buying one large one! Always look for the price per ounce on the shelf. If your grocery store does not list the cost per ounce, take a calculator with you when shopping so you can figure out the cost per ounce or serving.

The High and Low

Look up and down, high and low. The most expensive—and profitable—items are placed at eye level. The generic, store brands or other good deals are frequently placed high on the shelf or low to the ground.

Bargain or Regular Price?

Beware of "sale" items on the ends of aisles. Many times these items are not on sale at all. Manufacturers have found that sales increase by as much as 600 percent when the item is placed on the end of an aisle. Know your prices and be sure this is really a bargain before you stock up. Also compare the price to other brands on the shelf in the regular aisle. You may be able to find a better bargain that is not "on sale."

Not a Bargain

All nonfood items, such as kitchen gadgets, health and beauty aids, cleaning supplies, and seasonal items, are priced very high at the grocery store. These are considered convenience items. Always purchase nonfood items at a discount store. Don't give in to temptation, even if the item seems reasonably priced. Unless you know for sure the item is on sale at a low price, skip these aisles and make a trip to a discount store to pick them up.

Check the Checker

Don't lose all your savings at the checkout! Pay close attention to prices as you shop, and watch closely as the cashier is ringing up your groceries. Some stores give you the item free if you find that the item scans at a different price from the shelf price. Don't assume that the scanner is perfect. If you pay attention you can find errors, and you can bet that they are not usually in your favor. In most discrepancies the pricing clerk will have increased the price in the computer before the shelf price has been changed.

Watch when produce is being rung up, too. One wrong code entered by the cashier can cost a bundle. One variety of red apples may cost 99 cents per pound, whereas another variety of red apples may cost $3.49 per pound. Check the price per pound on each produce item you purchase. Write down the prices on your grocery list if you cannot remember them all.

Food Tips to Lower Your Grocery Bill

Make your own inexpensive flavored pancake and waffle syrup: Stir 4 tablespoons of your favorite jam or preserves into 1 cup of corn syrup in a saucepan over low heat. Store any leftover syrup in the refrigerator.

Don't buy expensive instant oatmeal packages. Regular oatmeal cooks just as fast in the microwave and costs less than one fourth the price. Add your own spices and fruits to make flavored oatmeal.

When cooking, always measure ingredients. You will not only get consistent results with your recipes but save money, too. Most people will add about twice as much as needed when they do not measure. This means you will end up buying twice as much.

Don't buy expensive freezer tape; use ordinary masking tape. It works just as well as freezer tape at a fraction of the price. You can easily write on it with a permanent marker.

Make your own inexpensive flavored coffee by adding cocoa, cinnamon, or almond or vanilla flavoring. Or try stirring in a small chocolate mint candy for a low-cost flavored coffee.

For flavored teas, make a pitcher of iced tea and add ½ cup lemonade, punch, orange juice, or any other flavor drink you like. It's much cheaper than the expensive flavored teas.

When a recipe calls for wine, you can substitute cranberry or grape juice. For white wine, simply substitute apple juice. The juice saves money, tastes great, and you probably already have some on hand!

To "save" a dry cake, poke holes in the top with a toothpick and pour a small amount of fruit juice in the holes.

If bananas are starting to turn brown before you can eat them, put them in the refrigerator. The cold air will kill cells in the skin and the skin will turn brown, but the banana inside will stay fresh for several more days.

Send away for free recipe booklets or calendar offers. Even if you have to send in a few proofs of purchase, it is worth the effort, because with most offers you'll get several dollars' worth of free coupons.

Look for Bonus Items

When shopping for health and beauty aids, look at the back of the shelf to see if any of the products have some sort of bonus. A bonus can be in the form of an instant coupon attached to the product, more of the product for the same price, or a freebie such as a toothbrush or razor attached to the package. Many times these bonus packages are pushed to the back of the shelf so the store can get rid of the regular-sized products without the bonus. It pays to search the shelves.

It Makes Cents

Clipping coupons can save you money, but you must be careful when using them to make sure you are getting the best value. Manufacturers often give away coupons for some of their most expensive products. Always comparison shop; you may be able to find a better deal without a coupon.

Double Dilemma

Not as many stores offer discounts of double the coupon value as they did a few years ago. If you like to use coupons, call all the local grocery stores and discount drug stores and ask if and when they offer double coupon discounts. Some stores will offer double coupon discounts on a slow day of the week, such as Tuesday or Wednesday. Others will offer double coupon discounts on the first Tuesday of the month. If you take a few minutes to find out when and where the double-coupon days are, you can really increase your savings.

Always take your coupon file with you when shopping. If you run across a terrific unadvertised special, you can use your coupon now, when the price is low.

Stock Up on Supplies

Use coupons to stock up on items such as toilet paper, shampoo, detergent, and any other nonperishable items when the store has a special price and you have several coupons. If you can get a product for practically nothing, it is worth stocking up and storing it for a while, because you know that your family will eventually use it.

Which Is the "Economy" Size?

You may think buying in large quantities is the cheapest way to go, but when shopping with coupons, many times the smallest size is the cheapest per ounce. Getting several small bottles for just a few pennies or even free is better than using the same coupons to buy several large bottles that will cost $1 or $2 each. Always take a calculator with you when shopping with coupons so you can figure out the cost per ounce after deducting the coupon.

Q. Wouldn't food prices be cheaper if the manufacturers quit printing coupons?

A. Coupons are part of the manufacturers' advertising budgets. If they didn't spend the money on coupons, they would undoubtedly spend it on television, radio, or print advertising. If they issue the coupons, at least you have a chance to save some money.

Ask the grocery store manager if he or she will accept another store's coupons or advertised specials. Many stores do this but don't advertise the fact.

Don't Buy Something Just Because You Have a Coupon

Many coupons are printed for highly packaged convenience foods that will not be bargain priced even with the coupon. Don't even bother clipping that type of coupon.

Using coupons is an easy way to battle the ever increasing cost of feeding a family. Think of your coupon savings as a hobby and make a game out of it. Whether you are a serious "coupon queen" or just an occasional clipper, your savings add up faster than you think. Don't get discouraged; if you save just $5 per week with coupons, that's $260 per year.

Get Satisfaction

If you have a problem with a product you have bought or it just does not meet your standards, call the company's toll-free number. Look for it on the back of the product; if it is not listed on the product, call long-distance information at 1-800-555-1212 to get the number. Or you can write the company a letter to explain the problem. Be upbeat, but let them know you were disappointed with the product. Most companies are very oriented toward customer service. They want to make you happy. Companies will send a refund and/or or replacement coupons for almost any reasonable complaint.

REFUND A BUNDLE (OF CASH!)

Using coupons and refunds go hand in hand. You can save with coupons, but refunds bring the savings up from cents to dollars. The average cash refund is about $1.50, though many are worth $2 to $5. Manufacturers generally offer three types of refunds: cash rebates, free merchandise, and product discounts.

Cash rebates are exactly that. Buy the required product, follow the directions, and the manufacturer will mail you a check for the amount of the refund.

Free merchandise can be anything from glasses with the company logo on them to video games. If you use the product anyway, you might as well collect the merchandise. Some make excellent gifts.

Product discounts can be structured so that if you buy one or more products, you get a coupon for another of the same product. Sometimes the offer is for another product— if you buy four boxes of chicken soup mix, you get a $2-off coupon for fresh chicken.

You can find refund forms in the same places that you find coupons—the coupon inserts in the Sunday newspaper and magazines. But the best place to find refund offers is at the store, sometimes attached to the product itself or displayed on the shelf. Most grocery stores and discount stores post refunds that are currently available on a bulletin board. Check the refund bulletin board each time you shop to see if a new refund is available for a product you plan to buy.

When sending away for a refund, always follow the directions exactly. If you do not include all the required items, you will not get a refund. Because some refund offers will not mail refund checks to a post office box, it's best to have any refund checks mailed to a street address instead of a post office box.

REFUND A BUNDLE (OF CASH!)

Most refund offers require you to send in:

1. The original refund offer (copies are not accepted).

2. The original cash register receipt for the required purchase.

3. Proof of purchase from the package, generally the UPC code.

If you buy several items with refund offers on the same shopping trip, ask the cashier to ring up the refund items separately. You will have original cash register receipts to send for each refund.

Look for refund offers on nonfood items, too. Health and beauty aids often have refund offers. Even socks and underwear manufacturers can offer refunds for up to $10. Small kitchen appliances or other accessories also have refund offers from time to time.

Act quickly when you participate in a refund. Deadlines are typically short, and if you put off sending in for the refund, you could either misplace the needed receipt and proof of purchase or miss the deadline.

Refunding involves some time and cost. Finding the refund offers, filling out the forms, and obtaining the proofs of purchase can be time-consuming. You'll also spend money on envelopes and postage stamps. But in most cases, the savings are well worth the effort—and if you are going to buy the product anyway, the refund is money in the bank!

WINTER BEST BUYS CALENDAR

December

Apples, broccoli, Brussels sprouts, chicken, cranberries, grapefruit, lamb, oranges, oysters, pork, sweet potatoes, tangelos, tangerines, turkey, turnips, winter squash, used cars, Christmas and party items, hats, infants' needs, boys' suits, men's clothing.

January

Beef, broccoli, Brussels sprouts, chicken, eggs, grapefruit, oranges, pork, rhubarb, turnips, Christmas decorations, linens and towels, bedding, holiday clothes, women's clothes, gifts, stationery, radios, appliances, china, home furnishings, art supplies, bicycles, costume jewelry, electronic equipment, lingerie.

February

Apples, broccoli, chicken, fish, oranges, oysters, rhubarb, scallops, turnips, housewares, men's clothing, shoes, toys, winter clothing, coats, leather goods, large appliances, bedding, furniture, curtains, sportswear, toys, lamps, rugs, carpeting.

HEAT IT UP!

For most parts of the United States, winter means it's time to turn on the heater. According to the U. S. Department of Energy, about half of the residential energy costs in America are used in heating and cooling our houses. Try these ways to save energy and reduce your heating bill during the cold winter months.

Don't turn on your heat until you have to. When the evenings start to get cool, wear warmer clothes and add an extra blanket or two.

Clean or replace the filter in your forced-air heating system every month.

Keep draperies and shades open during sunny days to allow the warming sun rays inside. Close them at night to help keep cold air out.

> He that burns logs that cost nothing is twice warmed.
>
> Benjamin Franklin
> (1706-1790)

Hot air rises. In a room with a high ceiling, a ceiling fan on low speed can keep heat lower in the room without creating a feeling of cold drafts. During the winter your fan should be rotating counterclockwise at the lowest speed. This will bring the warm air down from the ceiling to make the room feel warmer. The cost of operating a ceiling fan is minimal.

To keep cold air outside, caulk and weather-strip all doors and windows. You'll probably spend less than $50 in materials, and you could net a savings of about 10 percent on your heating costs.

Look for cracks, both inside and outside, that allow cold air into the house. Likely places are around window frames, air conditioning units, and vents and wherever pipes enter the house. Fill the cracks or holes with caulk to keep your heat inside and your utility costs down.

House Audit

Before you start to add insulation or upgrade your water heater or furnace, give your local power company a call. You may be surprised at their willingness to help with the process. Many local power companies offer a free walk-through energy audit, and they may even be able to help with the costs of a home energy fix-up. Financial help such as rebates or monthly discount credits may be available for various improvements. They may be able to perform a duct check and share in the costs of improvements. Taking the time to schedule an energy audit is time well spent.

Tune Up and Save

To keep your heating system working efficiently, have it serviced at least once every other year. A professional tune-up can save you as much as 10 percent on your winter fuel bills. Plan ahead and have it serviced before the cold weather sets in. Once the frigid air hits and everyone turns on the heat, servicemen will be swamped with emergency repairs.

Outlets Let It Out!

Electrical outlets around the house need to be sealed with inexpensive gaskets to prevent heat loss. You can find these gaskets at any hardware store. This is a simple project that anyone can do. Don't forget to turn off the power before installing the gaskets.

HEAT IT UP!

More Moisture

The humidity level in your house plays a large part in how comfortable the temperature feels. If you have static electricity in your house or your family seems to have dry throats and nasal passages, the air is probably too dry. Add a house plant or keep a bowl or pan of water out. The extra humidity will make you feel warmer without turning up the thermostat.

Weather the Storm

Storm windows and doors are worth the extra bother and expense. Energy experts estimate that by adding storm windows and doors, you may be able to slash as much as 15 percent from your heating and cooling costs.

Fireplace Facts

In many houses fireplaces are net energy losers. But if you follow a few of these tips, you can enjoy the crackling fire without paying a high price.

Build small, steady fires instead of large, roaring fires. Smaller fires are more efficient at warming the house—less energy goes up the chimney.

Invest in a glass door for the front of your fireplace. It's a real energy saver.

Once the fire in your fireplace is completely out, close the damper immediately. An open damper will let the warmed air in your house escape through the chimney.

Check your damper to see if there is a gap when it's closed. Some dampers leave a gap of an inch or more. This gap allows heated and cooled air to escape through the chimney. Close the gap with insulation or a flue plug when your fireplace is not in use.

CLOTHING COUNTS

Your body gives off heat. Dressing for cold weather can make you more comfortable without added energy costs.

- Close-woven fabrics add at least a half degree in warmth to your body.
- Slacks are warmer than skirts or dresses by at least one degree.
- A light long-sleeved sweater adds almost two degrees in warmth.
- A heavy long-sleeved sweater adds about four degrees.
- Two lightweight sweaters add about five degrees in warmth, because the air between them serves as insulation to keep in more body heat.

Timing Is Everything

One of the easiest ways to save on your annual heating bill is to set back the thermostat before bedtime or when everyone will be out of the house for several hours. Energy experts estimate that you can save up to 15 percent on your annual heating costs by turning the thermostat down five degrees while your family sleeps. You can manually do this each evening, or you can invest in a clock thermostat. Unlike humans, the clock thermostat won't forget. You can also set it to warm the house back up to the normal temperature before your family gets up in the morning or gets home from work or school. Clock thermostats are easily installed and cost from about $30 to more than $300 for a very sophisticated model. A lower-priced model will do the trick and save money.

SAVE, SAVE, SAVE

The goal of a frugal lifestyle is not just to make ends meet, but to have enough money left over to save for the future.

Start Small

Starting a savings account is one of those things that's so easy to put off. You can always find somewhere to spend the extra few dollars left at the end of the month. To make it easy on yourself, start with a small amount—even $10 or $25 per month is worth saving. Continue to make small payments to your savings account every payday.

Eight Tips for Building a Savings Account

1. Include a savings "bill" along with your other monthly bills. Make a payment to your savings account each month. If your budget is tight, start with a small amount and try to increase it over time. Just $50 a month will add up to $600 in a year—and that's before adding in interest.

2. After a car loan or other installment loan is paid off, continue to make the "payments" to your savings account.

3. Save all your loose change in a jar; whenever the jar is full, roll up the coins and deposit them into savings. Always pay only with bills so the change will add up quickly. When your purchase is $4.02, you'll have 98 cents to put into the change jar.

4. When you get a raise in pay, have the additional money go directly to your savings account. It's money you didn't have before, so you won't miss it now. Put any bonus checks or overtime pay into your savings account.

5. Deposit all rebate checks and money saved using coupons into your savings account.

6. Put all found money—the money found in the laundry and under sofa cushions—into the change jar for savings.

7. To jump-start a savings account, have a yard sale. Deposit the profit into your savings account. This will get you off on the right foot and in the habit of saving money.

8. If you receive an income tax refund, deposit it into savings.

Formula to Double Your Money

With compound interest, your money grows faster than you think. You can calculate how long it will take to double your money by dividing 72 by the annual interest rate on your savings account. For example, if your money is earning 6 percent interest, it will take 12 years to double. (72 divided by 6 equals 12.)

Interest rate	Number of years
3%	24
4%	18
5%	14.4
6%	12
7%	10.29
8%	9
9%	8
10%	7.2

SAVE, SAVE, SAVE

Emergency Fund

When your savings start to mount up, you'll want to invest them in something that pays more interest than a simple savings account does. But before you even start to think about investing money, you will want an emergency fund. You should have enough money to pay all your monthly expenses for at least three months. Keep this savings in a regular bank account or a money market mutual fund, where you can get to it in case of a financial emergency. An emergency fund should be able to pay for unexpected expenditures or get you through a short period of unemployment.

Cash Out the Credit Cards

After you have established an emergency fund, the next step is to pay off your credit card debt. It's crazy to put money into investments while you're paying 18 percent or more in interest on your credit cards. Over the long term, few investments return that much.

Savings on the House

Did you know that if you take out a $100,000 mortgage for 30 years at 7.5 percent interest, you'll end up paying more than a quarter of a million dollars— $251,716, to be exact? Paying extra on the principal of your mortgage is one of the best ways to "invest" your money. Generally speaking, you can reduce a 30-year mortgage to 25 years just by making one extra payment per year. Even sending an extra $50 principal payment each month will knock years off your mortgage and save you thousands of dollars in interest. In addition to setting aside retirement investments, concentrate on paying off your mortgage before you start looking into other investments.

It's true that when your mortgage is paid off, you'll lose the annual tax deduction. But you will always be better off not having a house payment than you would be having an interest deduction. Just think of the freedom you would have without a mortgage. You could get by very comfortably on much less money.

The biggest downside to paying off your mortgage is that your money is not liquid. In the case of an emergency, you can't quickly cash out your house as you could a money market account. That's one reason why you keep your three months' expenses in the bank. If you really worry about getting access to the value of your house, you can set up a home equity line of

---

QUICK PAYOFF

On a 30-year, $100,000 mortgage at 7.5 percent interest, the monthly payment is $699. The following chart shows how many years early you would pay off your mortgage, and how much interest you would save, if you added more to the principal payment.

An extra payment of...	Would retire your mortgage in...	And would save in interest...
$22	27 years	$18,036
30	26 years	24,192
40	25 years	29,940
107	20 years	58,200
228	15 years	84,780
488	10 years	109,200

---

credit. The rates can be very attractive on home equity loans, and some banks don't charge any fees to open up the line of credit.

Fifteen-Year Mortgage

When you buy a house or refinance your mortgage, think long and hard about a 15-year mortgage. You'll pay more each month, but you'll save tens of thousands of dollars in interest and get out of the mortgage trap in half the time. In addition, generally you can expect interest rates to be ½ to 1 point lower for a 15-year mortgage, which will save you even more money.

Q. What is a biweekly mortgage? I received a notice from a company urging me to sign up for one. The notice said I could save thousands or even tens of thousands of dollars in interest charges.

A. When you have a biweekly mortgage, the lending company debits your bank account every two weeks. The amount debited is equal to one-half of your regular monthly mortgage payment. Instead of making 12 monthly payments per year, you make 26 biweekly payments, which equates to 13 monthly payments each year. The biweekly mortgage will give you the discipline to prepay your mortgage. If you want to pay off your mortgage early and do not have the willpower to do it, a biweekly mortgage is a painless way to go.

Having a company other than your original lending institution convert your mortgage into a biweekly mortgage does have problems. One problem is the up-front fee the company will charge, approximately $500. Companies that offer to convert your mortgage to a biweekly one draft your bank account twice a month and make interest on your money until they make the mortgage payment for you. You will save money because you make an extra mortgage payment every year. But the real winner is the company, because they make interest on your money on top of the up-front fee.

You can save all the up-front fees and the hassles of a middleman handling your money by asking your lending institution to draft your account directly every two weeks. Most lenders can draft your account as if it were a biweekly mortgage without charging you any fees. By doing this, you are forced into the discipline of paying off your mortgage early without the feeling of deprivation.

A small house is better than a large mortgage.

Anonymous

Rush to Refinance

If you find that mortgage interest rates have dropped more than 2 percentage points lower than your mortgage rate, you can save money by refinancing your mortgage. Before you go through the bother and expense of getting a new loan, try to renegotiate your existing mortgage. A loan officer could reduce the interest rate, which would lower your monthly costs while keeping the balance and term of your original loan. It's a simple process for both the lender and the borrower, and the best news is you avoid paying closing costs.

CREDIT AND BANKING TIPS

Credit cards can be a curse or a blessing, expensive or cheap, depending on how they are used. Using credit cards is a way of life today. Even if you don't like using credit cards, you need to have at least one. Without a credit card it can be hard to rent a car, buy an airline ticket, or order anything by phone or on the Internet.

A credit card is different from a charge card. When you use a credit card, such as Visa or Mastercard, you are borrowing the money from the credit card issuer, and you can pay it back in installments. You are charged interest from around 10 percent to as much as 19.8 percent on your unpaid balance. When you use a charge card, such as American Express, you must pay the bill in full when it comes in. Charge cards and some credit cards levy an annual fee to carry the card.

Two Are Enough

If you have a wallet packed full of credit cards, you may be paying much more in interest and fees than you realize for the cards. A large number of credit cards also means a greater exposure to loss or theft, more bills to be paid, extra bookkeeping and postage, and confusion. A lost or stolen wallet will make you realize the folly of having tons of credit cards. Even if you do not use them all, you could be turned down for a loan if you have a large line of credit available to you. Use a maximum of two bank credit cards, one card with no annual fee for those charges you will pay off in full each month, and one card with a low interest rate for bills that you want to pay off in installments.

The truly frugal will save in advance for large purchases and never pay an interest charge.

Give Me Grace

Choose credit cards that have a grace period (the period of time before interest charges start being added to your account) of at least 24 days. Some credit cards start charging interest on the day you make the purchase. If you have a card that doesn't offer a grace period, you'll end up paying interest on every purchase you make, even if you pay the bill as soon as it arrives.

Many people are confused about how their grace period works. Credit card holders may think they will not be charged interest on new purchases as long as they have made the minimum payment. In fact, for most cards you have a grace period for new purchases only if you have no outstanding balance on your card. You must pay your bill in full to avoid paying interest on new purchases.

Consolidate

If you have several credit cards or just one high-interest credit card with a large balance you are working to pay off, you can save money by "refinancing" your credit card debt. Apply for a low-interest credit card and transfer your high-interest debt to the low-interest credit card and start saving. According to Credit Counseling Services, the average consumer can save $200 per year by consolidating credit card debt to one low-interest card.

The Cost of Credit

Before you say "charge it," consider how much you will actually end up paying for the item. Look at the

How much $500 Really Costs			
Interest rate	**6 months**	**12 months**	**24 months**
19.8%	$547	$585	$637
18%	$542	$577	$622
16%	$537	$568	$606
14%	$532	$559	$590
12%	$528	$550	$575

chart above to see how much a $500 purchase will cost by the time you pay it off.

If you saved the $500 first, not only could you pay the bill right away, but also you would have the interest the $500 earned in the bank!

Don't be trapped into making only the minimum payment on your balance. The minimum payment is typically less than 3 percent of what you owe. If you charge $2,000 and pay only the minimum each month, it can take as long as 30 years to pay it off—and you will pay thousands in interest.

Retailers' Cards

Credit cards offered by oil companies, home improvement stores, and department stores generally carry some of the highest interest rates around. It is not unusual for the APR (annual percentage rate) charged on these cards to be 18 to 22 percent or even higher. Most credit cards of this type offer a grace period of 20 to 30 days, so if you pay off the balance each month, you shouldn't be charged interest. But even if you pay off the charges each month, you still have the additional bookkeeping and postage of paying a separate bill each month. Most retailers will also accept other credit or charge cards. The only advantage to using the department store's card is that you will receive the store's catalog.

> Credit is a clever financial trick that enables us to spend what we haven't got.
>
> Anonymous

Too Good to be True!

If a low-interest credit card offer seems too good to be true, it probably is too good to be true. The low interest rate can be bait—often the low rate will last for only six months to one year, and you may not have a grace period before interest starts being charged to your account. Your interest rate could skyrocket after the initial "free period," and your annual fees could be as high as $100 per year. Read the fine print if you see an offer for an extremely low interest rate. If you discover that you signed up for a card that charges a much higher rate after six months, pay off the balance and switch to a cheaper card after the lower-rate period ends.

Make Mine No-fee, Please

If you have a credit card that offers a good interest rate but charges an annual fee, you may be able to get the fee waived. Credit card companies are very aware of the competition, and they know that many no-fee cards are available. When you get the monthly statement with the annual fee on it, talk to a customer service representative. Tell them that you are happy with the credit card but unhappy with the annual fee. If you have a good credit standing, chances are very good that they will waive the fee for you. If your credit card will not waive the annual fee, shop for a no-fee card.

Along with the annual fee, most credit cards levy a fee if you charge more than your limit. They will also charge a late-payment fee if your check doesn't come by the date printed on your statement.

For $4 you can get a list of low-interest, no-fee cards. Write to:

Bankcard Holders of America
560 Herndon Parkway
Suite 120
Herndon, VA 22070

Rebate Cards

Recently co-branded cards have become available. With some credit cards, you can earn frequent-flier miles, usually one mile for each dollar you charge. Other co-branded cards allow you to earn rebate dollars toward a new car or toward purchases of gasoline. To determine if these are good deals, weigh the annual fee and the interest rate against the rebate you're getting. Also bear in mind your spending patterns and how long it will take to earn the rebate. A typical credit card user charges only around $2,500 per year.

The Price of Gold

Premium "gold" or "platinum" credit cards have a higher credit limit, but they also carry a premium price. The annual fee on these cards can be as low as $35 or as high as $300 per year! These cards are designed for vanity and snob appeal. In addition to the perception of status and the high credit limits, these cards offer additional benefits or services. Most regular credit cards allow you to increase your credit limit if you need to. As for the additional benefits, look at what's offered and see which benefits, if any, are really of value to you. Chances are good that you won't use most of the additional benefits. Plus, the most popular benefits are generally offered with regular credit cards in addition to the premium charge cards.

Q. I am working to pay off a credit card balance. Which is better, to take money out of my savings account to help bring down the balance, or to leave the money in the account to draw interest?

A. You can save quite a bit of credit card interest by using part of your savings to pay off the credit card debt. You're losing 15 percent a year if you have a savings account earning 4 percent interest and a credit card costing 19 percent interest. It's better to go ahead and pay off the debt—but you must be very disciplined about paying back the "loan" from your savings account. When you are through making payments to the credit card company, make a payment to your savings account each month.

If you can't pay your credit card charges in full every month, pay off the cards with the highest interest rate first. Once you get the cards paid off, cancel the cards with the highest rates and stick with one low-interest, no-fee card.

CREDIT AND BANKING TIPS

Say No to Cash Advances

Most cards will now allow you cash advances at automatic teller machines or will send you checks you can write for a cash advance. Don't do it. You will be charged interest from the very day you take the cash advance, and you may also be charged a fee. It's much better to take the money from your bank account. If your credit card company sends you an offer to waive the fee on a cash advance, check to see if it is also waiving the first month's interest.

Free Credit Check

It's a good idea to review your credit report once a year. An error on your credit report can cause you to be turned down for a car or home loan—or at least it can slow down the approval process while you try to clear up the error. You can get a free look at your credit report from the nation's largest credit reporting firm. TRW allows consumers to request one copy each year without charge. (Other credit firms charge $8 or more for each report.) To get your free credit report, send a written request with your name, address, social security number, and a copy of your driver's license or other photo identification. Call 1-800-392-1122 for more information, or send a written request to:

TRW Information Systems
National Consumer Assistance Center
P.O. Box 2350
Chatsworth, CA 91313-2350

Bank the Savings

Shopping for a bank, whether to open a checking or savings account or to apply for a loan, should be approached the same way as shopping for anything else.

Decide what services are important to you and comparison shop several banks. Services and costs can vary significantly from one bank to another. Even at the same bank, different types of accounts will carry different charges. Some bank accounts have no service charge but charge a fee for each check. Some accounts charge for use of an automated teller machine (ATM). Most banks will waive some or all of the fees if you keep a minimum monthly balance, and the minimum can range from $100 to several thousand, depending on the type of account. Banks are becoming ever more creative in thinking up new charges, so it also pays to read the inserts that come with your monthly statement. They could be announcing a change in fees.

> *Put not your trust in money, but put your money in trust.*
>
> Dr. Oliver Wendell Holmes
> (1809-1894)

If you find a bank that waives the service charge if you maintain a certain amount in your account, make sure it assesses its service charge based on average monthly balances. Avoid banks that base charges on minimum monthly balances. If your balance drops below the minimum for even one day, you'll be charged a fee.

Ask your bank to consider all accounts when calculating your average monthly balance. If you have a savings account or a certificate of deposit, you may be able to keep a lower balance in your checking account without having to pay a fee.

Look for a bank that does not charge a fee for using an automated teller machine. Charges for using an ATM can range from 50 cents to $3 for each transaction. Some banks allow you to use their own ATMs at no charge but charge you for using other banks' ATMs.

You may be eligible for a no-fee checking account even if you aren't a senior citizen and cannot maintain a high minimum balance. Many banks now offer free checking to customers with an outstanding loan balance greater than $12,000. It pays to ask!

When applying for a loan, compare costs other than just the interest rate. Many banks charge an application fee or processing fee; if one bank charges $25 and another bank charges $175, the difference in interest rates may be more than made up by additional fees.

If you have banked at the same location for many years or you are a senior citizen, ask the branch manager what special services are offered for seniors or preferred customers. Goodies may include lower interest rates on loans, a free checking account, free checks, a no-fee credit card, free traveler's checks, a free safe-deposit box, or free accident insurance.

Look for the Union Label

Instead of using a bank, think about joining a credit union. Credit unions are nonprofit financial institutions that people can join if they have some kind of common bond. Some are open to people who work in a certain industry or for a certain employer. Credit unions offer the same services that banks do, but because they are nonprofit cooperatives, they usually pay higher interest rates on deposits and charge lower interest rates on loans. They also typically have lower service charges.

Bank accounts of up to $100,000 are insured by the Federal Deposit Insurance Corporation. Accounts in most credit unions are also insured up to $100,000, but by the National Credit Union Administration. Your money is just as safe in a good credit union as it is in a good bank.

Because credit unions are also open to relatives of people belonging to the group, many Americans are eligible to join but don't know it. Call the National Credit Union Administration at 202-682-9600 for a list of credit unions you might be eligible to join.

Checks on the Cheap

You can save money by ordering your checks through the mail. An order of checks from the bank generally costs between $15 and $18 for a box of 200. You'll get the same amount from a mail-order service for $5 to $6. But before ordering, ask your bank if they will match the mail-order price; some banks will. Even after you pay the shipping cost, you're still many dollars ahead. Call for a free catalog.

Current	1-800-533-3973
Artistic Checks	1-800-224-7621
Checks in the Mail	1-800-733-4443

You can also watch advertising flyers for special offers. Frequently one of these companies will offer a special price for first-time orderers.

Certificates of Deposit

A certificate of deposit (CD) will almost always pay more interest than a regular savings account. You'll usually need at least $500 or $1000 to open one. When you buy a CD, you agree to leave the money in the bank for a specified amount of time. It can be three months, six months, one year, or several years. Typically, the longer the time to maturity, the higher the interest rate. If you withdraw money from a CD before it matures, you'll pay a substantial penalty. Before you open one, make sure that you won't need the money before it matures.

When your CD matures, unless you instruct the bank otherwise, the money plus interest will roll over at a rate of interest that may be less than or more than the original rate of interest. To make sure you are not locking your money into a low rate of interest, you can "ladder" your CDs. This means buying CDs of different maturities. If you have $5,000 to invest, for example, you might buy a five-year CD at 6 percent, a two-year CD at 5.6 percent, a one-year CD at 5.3 percent, a six-month CD at 5 percent, and a three-month CD at 4.7 percent. If interest rates go up, you can buy a new long-term CD with the money from your three-month CD. If they go down, you're still earning good rates from your long-term CDs.

You don't have to buy a CD at your own bank. Check listings in the newspaper to find the highest yield available. You can even open a CD in another state. *The Wall Street Journal* and some business magazines publish lists of high-yielding CDs across the country.

INVESTMENT STRATEGIES

Bank accounts and CDs pay a guaranteed rate of return. Investing in stocks and mutual funds can make more money, but the rate of return is not guaranteed. You can make less or even lose money. Over time, however, the stock market has outperformed other investments. If you will not need your money for at least ten years and you have already accumulated your emergency fund, you may want to think about investing in the stock market.

You can do this by buying stocks directly through a broker. If you do this, you should do careful research into the company you are investing in, comparing balance sheets and profit statements. Don't blindly follow the advice of the broker—know what you are investing in. Make sure your investments are diversified and not concentrated in one industry.

An easier way that millions of Americans have embraced is to invest in mutual funds. Today there are more mutual funds than stocks listed on the New York Stock Exchange. When you buy shares in a mutual fund, you are pooling your money with other investors and letting the professional fund manager decide how to invest it. The typical fund invests in dozens of securities and may be diversified across several industries. The mutual fund has millions or even billions of dollars in its coffers—the largest fund, Fidelity Magellan, has a capitalization of more than $50 billion.

When an investor buys 100 shares of stock at a certain price, he is buying them from another investor. The number of shares of stock available for purchase doesn't change unless the company issues more. The vast majority of mutual funds work differently. They take in money directly, and so the number of shares increase if more are sold. The share price is determined by dividing the total value of the fund's investments by the number of shares all the investors have. This price is called the net asset value, or NAV. If the fund's investments go up in value, the NAV rises. You can find the NAV for most mutual funds in the business section of the newspaper.

Types of Mutual Funds

Money market mutual funds invest in short-term money instruments. They are the least volatile of mutual funds; the value of a share is almost always $1. They often pay dividends that are higher than those of bank accounts, and some of them allow check-writing privileges.

Growth funds invest their assets in the stocks of companies that are expected to grow in value. The volatility of the fund depends on the stock market itself and on the investment style of the fund manager.

Growth-and-income funds invest in the stocks of companies that pay good dividends. The companies may also be expected to grow.

Bond funds invest in bonds issued by corporations, municipalities, or governments. Bond funds are not normally as volatile as stock funds, but if interest rates go up, the price of bonds goes down.

Balanced funds invest in a mixture of stocks and bonds.

Asset allocation funds invest in stocks, bonds, and cash instruments. They change the relative proportions allocated to these different investment forms depending on market conditions or the economy.

Index funds seek to mirror the activity of a stock index, such as the Standard & Poor 500. This index is an average of 500 large companies.

International funds invest in foreign securities. Investing in overseas companies can be very profitable, but the risks are also great. Unstable political conditions can affect foreign markets, and the fluctuations in currency rates of exchange can eat into the fund's profits.

Load or No-load

Some mutual funds are sold with an up-front sales charge, or "load." This charge ranges from 3 percent to 6 percent. Certain classes of funds charge a back-end load, which is a sales charge you pay when you sell your shares. Usually this back-end load decreases with time, so that if you hold your shares for years, you won't be charged when you sell. Many mutual funds, however, are "no-load" funds that don't charge a sales fee. At first glance it would seem foolish to invest in a load fund when so many no-load funds are available, but some of the top-performing funds are load funds. You have to study the activity of the fund and know what you are investing in.

When you change jobs, don't be tempted to spend the money in your retirement account. As soon as your employer pays out your retirement, roll it over into an individual retirement account (IRA) and keep making regular deposits.

How to Decide?

Choosing among more than 6,000 mutual funds can seem like a daunting task, but you can start narrowing the choices down bit by bit. First decide on the type of fund you want to invest in. Start reading books and magazines on investing to educate yourself. The most widely quoted source of information on mutual funds is Morningstar, Inc. Your local library probably has Morningstar reports on file. From these reports, focus on funds with strong records for the long term, such as five or ten years. This year's hot fund could be next year's dud. Notice the minimum investment required—some funds ask for a minimum of only $500, but others require $10,000 or even more. Read about the investment style of the fund to make sure you are comfortable with it.

When you have narrowed the field to just a few funds, call each one and ask for a prospectus. This is a statement of the fund's objectives and what the fund may or may not invest in. Read it very carefully. Make sure that you understand what the fund is invested in before you buy shares.

How to Invest

Some mutual funds are sold through brokers, and some are sold through banks. It is very important to distinguish between a bank account or CD and a mutual fund bought from a bank. Bank accounts of up to $100,000 are insured by the Federal Deposit Insurance Corporation. Mutual funds, even those sold by a bank, are not insured.

You can also invest in the mutual fund directly, by asking for a prospectus and an application. The fund will send you statements of your account at periodic intervals.

Many funds will allow automatic periodic investments. This is an excellent way to build your nest egg. You can ask the fund, for example, to deduct $100 from your checking account on the 15th of every month and purchase additional shares.

Safety First

Probably the safest investment available is in Treasury securities, although the rate of return can be less than that of other investments. The United States government issues Treasury notes that are intermediate (mature in two to ten years) and long-term bonds that mature in 30 years. The government also issues T-bills—short-term investments maturing in three months to a year. If you buy Treasurys from a broker, you will pay a commission. The cheapest way to buy Treasurys is from any Federal Reserve Bank or through the Treasury Direct program. For information call the Bureau of the Public Debt at 202-874-4000.

> Money is better than poverty, if only for financial reasons.
>
> Woody Allen (b. 1935)

Your Best Return

If your company has a 401(k) plan, you can have money taken from your paycheck and put in the plan. Your money will be invested to grow tax-free until you retire. Even better, the amount you contribute each year is deducted from your taxable income. That means that right off the bat, your money is effectively earning a percentage equal to your tax bracket. What's more, many companies match your contribution, typically with 50 cents for every dollar you put in. You can't beat a 50-percent return on your money!

Start Young

Building a retirement account is making an investment in your future. It's never too early to start. If you are self-employed or your employer does not offer a retirement plan, start an individual retirement account (IRA) and put up to $2,000 into it every year. It will grow tax-free until retirement, and depending on your income level and whether you have another pension plan, you might be able to deduct your contribution from your income at tax time.

If you start saving $2,000 per year at age 20 and earn an average of 5 percent interest, by age 65 you'll have $317,400. But if you wait until you're 40 and invest $5,000 per year at the same 5 percent interest, you'll have just $233,635 at 65, even though you saved an extra $3,000 each year. The moral of the story is to start saving at an early age. Small savings, when put away religiously, can add up to a comfortable retirement. You'll never be sorry.

BIG-TICKET BUYING

Since appliances are a large expenditure, spend some effort to avoid spending more money than you need to.

Consider the costs versus the benefits of buying an appliance that offers more features than you really need. All the fancy bells and whistles sound good during the sales pitch, but will you really use them? A more basic model would probably suit your needs at a much lower price. Look around for the basic model; it may be tucked away, since salespeople want to sell the higher-priced models.

Don't buy gadget appliances that you will seldom use. They waste money and take up space in your kitchen.

When shopping for large appliances, ask if floor models can be purchased at a reduced price. Look for closeouts when the newer models arrive. If you buy a discontinued model, make sure that parts, warranties, and service are still available.

Read and understand any terms, guarantees, and sales or service contracts when buying furniture and appliances. Choose a dealer that has been in business many years and that you know will stand behind what is sold.

In furniture, durability is more important than high fashion, if you want to save money. Look for signs of solid construction, and buy classic styles that won't quickly look dated. It is often more economical in the long run to pay a little more initially for good quality.

If you have children, be very careful to buy furniture that will stand up to wear and tear. Choose fabrics and colors that resist stain and clean easily.

Extended Warranties

When you buy an appliance, an electronic gadget, or a car, think twice before you sign up for the extended warranty. An extended warranty sounds like a good deal, because it stretches the amount of time you're entitled to free repairs or replacement if an item breaks down after the standard warranty has expired. But the odds are you'll be wasting your money.

In most cases, if the product has a defect, it will show up early, during the standard warranty period. A recent study found that 90 percent of consumers who buy extended warranties on electronic items and appliances never use them. The study found that many of those who do report problems simply need help with operating instructions. Extended warranties can add up to 30 percent to the cost of a product.

> *He who buys what he does not want will soon want what he cannot buy.*
>
> Anonymous

Cut down on appliance repairs by doing regular maintenance. Be sure to save the instruction booklet and sales receipt. Before having an appliance repaired, call the customer service department of the manufacturer (look for an 800 number) and ask questions about your problem. Many times they can walk you through the procedure to fix the problem, which can save you money and time.

Extended warranties for cars cost between $500 and $1,400. Typical factory warranties run from three to

How to Haggle

Most people bargain, negotiate, or haggle when they buy a car or shop at a garage sale or flea market. But you can and should bargain more often. Here are some tips to help you get the most for your money.

- Be prepared. Know the competitors' comparable prices. Making a ridiculously low offer will often offend the merchant and make him less willing to work with you.

- Smile and be pleasant. Let them know you are ready to buy, but not at the retail price.

- Always deal with someone in authority, such as the store owner or manager, and be discreet. Don't try to get them to reduce the price in front of other customers. Take the owner or manager off to the side and try to negotiate.

- The more you buy, the more leverage you have. For example, if you are remodeling your kitchen, buy all your appliances from the same dealer. He'll be much more willing to give you a discount.

- If you can't get the store to budge on the price, ask them to throw in some extras—disks for computers, paper for printers, blank tapes for cassette players.

- When making a large purchase, always ask for a 5-percent discount for paying with cash or a check. The store has to pay a fee to the credit card company for each transaction. They may be willing to give you a price break to avoid paying the credit card fee.

(continued)

How to Haggle *(continued)*

- Include sales tax in your offer, and be sure you make this clear by saying, "Tax included." For example, offer $500, tax included, for a television set. Of course the dealer will have to pay sales tax, but they will simply reduce the sales price to the correct pretax price.
- Keep in mind that the worst that can happen is the merchant will say no! Then you have to decide if you want to pay the price or try your luck haggling at another store.

---

seven years. Although factory warranties generally cover a long list of repairs, extended warranties for cars have a long list of repairs, parts, and labor that are exempt. It's doubtful that you'll get as much coverage from an extended car warranty as you think.

DISCOUNT DINING

Eating out is expensive. Even going out for a fast-food meal or ordering in a pizza can be costly; if you do it often, the expense adds up. If you really want to save big money, make it a habit to cook good meals and save an occasional restaurant meal for a once-in-a-while treat. Here are some ways to save when you do dine out.

• Be an early bird. Lunch will be much cheaper than dinner, and many times the menu will be the same. Early dining, typically 4 P.M. to 6 P.M., can be bargain-priced too. Find out when your favorite restaurant offers the best discounts and arrange your schedule to save the most money.

• Take out food instead of eating in restaurants. You save on drinks and tipping. Believe it or not, tips and drinks can add 25 percent or more to your total restaurant bill.

• Always ask about the daily specials. Be sure to ask the price, too. A "special" may have a special low price or it may be even higher than most entrees on the menu.

• You can slash your total bill at just about any restaurant simply by sharing a dish with the person you are eating with. Many restaurants will give you an extra plate for splitting the dinner. Even if they charge a dollar for the extra plate, you'll still save significantly. Chinese restaurants are notorious for serving large portions. One dinner can usually serve two people easily.

• Children and seniors may be entitled to discounts or, in some cases, free meals. Ask the waiter or waitress about senior or children's discounts, since many times they are not listed on the menu.

DISCOUNT DINING

• Look in the newspaper for buy-one-get-one-free restaurant coupons. Also pick up any local flyers or magazines that are printed for tourists. These publications often have super discounts for restaurants that are usually overlooked by locals.

• Drink water with your meal and save a dollar or two per person. If you must have a soft drink, ask for drinks without ice. The drinks will be cold, and you'll get more for your money. If the restaurant offers free refills on drinks, order the smallest or cheapest size and get as many refills as needed.

• Pass on the desserts. You can buy a whole pie or cake for the about the same price as one restaurant dessert.

• If your dinner is more than you can eat, ask to have the leftovers put in a doggie bag. You'll have an almost-free lunch tomorrow.

HOLIDAY BAKING

During the holidays most of us do more baking than usual. A homemade gift from the kitchen is always welcome. Look for special sales on baking staples such as flour, sugar, baking soda, vanilla, and chocolate chips. Grocery stores will offer a super-low price on a baking item such as flour as a loss leader to get you in the store. They hope you'll stop in for the bargain-priced flour and buy all your groceries while you're there. As you see these loss-leader sales on baking staples, stock up on them.

Shop discount stores for baking supplies. You can find some terrific buys on items such as spices, chocolate chips, coconut, marshmallows, and drinks.

Money-Saving Baking Tips

Sprinkle frosted cookies with packaged gelatin to add color instead of buying expensive colored sprinkles. Or make your own colored sugar sprinkles by shaking 2 to 3 tablespoons granulated sugar with 2 or 3 drops of food coloring in a zip-lock bag.

Don't throw away cookies that are burnt on the bottom. Instead, use a cheese grater to remove the burned portion. If the cookies crumble when you scrape off the burned part, save the crumbs to use as ice cream topping.

When baking a chocolate cake, add a little of the flour to the container you melted the chocolate in. The flour will get the last bit of chocolate out of the pan.

Don't throw away brown sugar that is as hard as a rock. Place a piece of fresh bread into the box or bag and close it tightly. The moisture from the bread will soften the brown sugar so it can easily be used.

THE HOLIDAY SEASON

'Tis the season—to overspend on gifts, wrapping, decorations, cards, foods, entertaining, travel, and holiday clothing. The list seems endless, and hidden expenses always seem to crop up. Financial experts say that during the holidays many people go overboard without even realizing it. You can have a festive, fun holiday season and still be frugal. Here are a few ways to help you keep expenses down without feeling like a Scrooge.

- Set a spending limit or budget. Know how much you can afford to spend, and then decide what you want to spend the money on. Make smart choices and cut corners on things that are the least important to you and your family.

- Start holiday shopping early and look for sales on the items on your list. If you are looking for a specific item, ask the department manager when it will be on sale. If they say the item will be on sale soon, many times you can get the item at the sale price without having to wait for the sale. Save your receipts, and if the item goes on sale within six months, ask for a refund of the difference.

- Buy family members gifts they need. A stepladder or a bathroom scale may not seem like a romantic gift, but if your loved one needs it, he or she will enjoy it much more than a necktie or another bottle of perfume.

- Pay cash or write checks for gifts. When you have to deduct the money from your checking account or hand over cash, you're less likely to overspend. If you charge all your purchases, you may be shocked when the bills arrive next year. Long after the gifts are opened, the charge card bills will still be due.

- Take an inventory of all your holiday items before you buy anything new. Your inventory will tell you what you are low on. You don't want to buy cards, bulbs, candles, or other items you already have on hand.
- Be creative with gift wrap. Use any wrap left over or saved from last year and look for other low-cost ways to wrap gifts.
- Instead of buying individual gifts within a group of people, such as work, church, and school, exchange names. If you have a large extended family, why not put all the names in a hat and have everyone buy just one gift? You'll save money, but everyone will still get a gift.

> November runs into December, December runs into Christmas, and Christmas runs into money.
>
> Anonymous

- Entertaining costs add up quickly. Plan get-togethers after dinner and serve desserts and coffee. A party can be festive and fun without being expensive. For a big family meal, have each family bring a different side dish or dessert. Everyone will enjoy the variety, and you'll cut your costs.
- Plan holiday travel early. If you are flying, buy airline tickets as soon as possible to get the lowest fares. Cheap seats are hard to come by during the holidays, and they sell out fast.
- Save on postage by mailing holiday postcards instead of cards. You'll have plenty of room to write a holiday message. Make homemade postcards out of

Christmas cards from last year. Cut the front of the cards (the part with the picture) to postcard size—4 inches by 5½ inches—and write the address and a holiday message on the back.

Let's Party

The holiday season is a time to get together with family and friends. You don't have to break the bank to have a fabulous party. Use these tips to make the most of holiday gatherings.

You don't have to buy expensive, disposable paper products just because you don't have enough matching china. Mix china from various patterns you own. Use a solid-color tablecloth to make the mixture of patterns look beautiful. The effect is eclectic and appealing.

If you do not have enough sets of matching silverware, wrap silverware in colorful cloth napkins and tie a ribbon around each set. Guests won't even notice that you have used several different sets of silverware. If you are serving buffet style, stand the wrapped silverware up in a large flower vase at the end of the line so guests can pick up a set.

For inexpensive decorations, wrap empty boxes and pictures on the walls in colorful holiday wrapping paper. Tie a pretty bow around the pictures and boxes. Spray-paint bare branches and pine cones and place them in baskets.

When you get out the good silverware to use for the holidays, instead of buying an expensive silver polish, use plain old white toothpaste. To clean tarnish off silver, coat the silver with toothpaste, then dip it in warm water, work the toothpaste into a foam, and rinse off. For stubborn stains use an old soft-bristled toothbrush.

To avoid wasting money buying bags of ice from the store, start making extra ice cubes several weeks before a holiday gathering. Store ice cubes in paper or plastic bags in the freezer. Make large cubes in plastic margarine containers to use in the punch bowl. The large blocks will keep the punch cold longer. You can also freeze grapes to float in punch.

Low-Cost and No-Cost Gifts

They say it's the thought that counts, and it's true. If you put a little thought into gift giving, you can save money and give a very special gift. Here are some ideas for you to try.

Family tree: Go to the library and trace your family tree. Most libraries have a genealogy department that will help you in your search. Frame the tree and give it to your immediate family members. You'll have put in a fair amount of time, but the gift won't cost much and it will be the talk of the holidays.

Heirloom gift: You probably have something you would like to be handed down from generation to generation. Why not surprise your child or grandchild this year and see them enjoy it?

Coupon book: A thoughtful, inexpensive gift for the holidays is a coupon book for services and favors. Children can make them for their parents or grandparents. What the coupons promise is limited only by your imagination. A teenager can make coupons to mow the lawn, shovel the sidewalk, or clean out the garage or attic for a parent or grandparent. This gift can be used long after the holidays have passed.

THE HOLIDAY SEASON

Collectibles: Search antique stores, flea markets, and garage sales for unusual items for someone with a special interest. Find an old cookbook for someone who loves to cook. Kitchen gadgets, old bottles, and buttons are just a few of the inexpensive items that make great gifts when given to the right person.

Homemade goodie container: Cover an oatmeal box with wrapping paper to hold homemade goodies. This works great for mailing cookies, taking goodies to work, or delivering them to nursing homes. The container is sturdy and looks pretty, and the recipient does not have to worry about returning the container.

Shelled nuts: If you have a nut tree in your yard or nearby, shell some nuts and put them in a jar. Decorate the jar with a colorful ribbon.

Care package: Buy several small inexpensive items instead of one large gift. A kitchen care package might include pot holders, dishcloths, paper towels, salt and pepper, and other miscellaneous kitchen items.

Homemade cookbook: Make a family cookbook of all the recipes that you treasure. Ask family members for the best recipes that everyone enjoys.

Manicure and facial: Give a gift of your time instead of your money. Offer to give your friend, mother, or sister a manicure or facial.

Bedtime stories: For a child or grandchild, make a cassette tape of fairy tales in your voice. A child will appreciate the tape, especially from a faraway relative.

Baby-sitting: Offer free baby-sitting as a gift. The adults will really appreciate their time alone, and the child will enjoy the special attention.

Photo album: Give a photo album full of memorable pictures. Be creative; include baby pictures or pictures from past generations. Be sure to write names and dates on each picture.

Calendar: If you're artistic, make a pretty calendar for the new year. Put important family dates on the calendar.

Bus or subway tokens: Any commuter would appreciate this useful gift.

Special song: Frame an old piece of sheet music in a pretty gold or black frame. A song with special meaning will be remembered for years to come. You can find old sheet music at antique stores and flea markets. The average cost is about a dollar per song.

Fleas for Christmas?

You may not think of shopping at the flea market for Christmas gifts, but if you are a careful shopper, you can find some great gifts at bargain prices. Some of these gifts may be perfect for someone on your shopping list.

An assortment of gift cards. Many flea markets have greeting cards for pennies. Add a book of stamps and a writing pen, and you have a welcome gift for anyone.

Hair ribbons and barrettes. Many flea markets have a large selection of hair ribbons and barrettes for less than half the original price. These make a perfect gift for many girls and young women.

Socks. Look for booths that sell close-out socks. They are discontinued styles and colors priced at a fraction of the original retail price.

Crafts. Crafters often sell their work at flea markets. You'll find everything for the country look. Some crafters do it to make money, but for others it's just a hobby. Prices will vary greatly from vendor to vendor.

Luggage and purses. Check prices at a local department store first to make sure you get a true bargain. You can find luggage at up to 75 percent off! A new suitcase or set of luggage is a perfect gift for a young couple, someone off to college, or anyone who travels frequently.

BATTERIES NOT INCLUDED!

When you buy a gift that displays those dreaded words "batteries not included," you can use these strategies for getting the most for your battery money.

When you shop for batteries, always check for expiration dates. Look for batteries that expire as far into the future as possible. If the store properly rotates merchandise, the newest batteries will be at the back of the shelf.

Batteries will last longer if you store them in the refrigerator. Batteries need to stay dry, so keep them in a airtight bag or container. Let the batteries reach room temperature before using them.

To prevent corrosion, remove batteries from devices that won't be used for a long time.

To get the most use out of batteries, don't mix old and new batteries or different brands of batteries in the same device.

Before using batteries, make sure the terminals are clean. When in doubt, clean them with a dry towel or pencil eraser.

Rechargeable batteries are a money-saving investment. Over time, both the batteries and the recharger pay for themselves.

When shopping for a recharger, look for one that won't overcharge if left plugged in too long. Also look for rechargeable batteries that offer a lifetime warranty to replace used batteries that will no longer hold a charge.

Tools. For someone who likes to work around the house, you can find bargain-priced tools at the flea market. Make sure you know exactly what tools the person wants.

Baskets and dried or silk flowers. Use the baskets as gift packages. Use the flowers to make inexpensive centerpieces and flower arrangements for yourself or for gifts.

Paperback books. Think cheap when buying paperback books. You can find them priced from 10 cents to $1 or more each. Any paperback less than 25 cents is a good buy.

Plants. For the plant lover, many flea markets offer the best prices in town. Shop other nurseries and garden departments to make sure you are getting the lowest price. Look in the other booths at the flea market for low-cost containers to use as pots. You are limited only by your imagination. Old pots, pans, and glassware make interesting containers for plants!

Wrap it Up!

Buy wrapping paper after the holidays when it's marked down to giveaway prices. If you wait long enough, you can find it for 75 percent to 80 percent off the original price. If you don't have any left over from last year, use some of these low-cost wrapping ideas.

Gift bags: Use the brown paper bags from the grocery store for gift bags. Let kids paint or color Christmas decorations on them. Tie the top together with red or green string. This is a lot cheaper than buying Christmas boxes and wrapping paper.

Gourmet gift: Save large and small bottles throughout the year. Wash them out and fill with a favorite coffee or potpourri. Once you tie a ribbon around the neck, it's wrapped and ready to go.

Bottle it: If you really want to drive your giftee crazy, put a small gift in a large bottle. First wrap the gift in crumpled-up paper and then place it inside the jar. You can also put confetti made from a hole punch in the jar for decoration.

Trash or treasure?: Wrap packages in any colorful paper you have. Try the comic section of the newspaper or the stock listings, old calendars, travel posters or brochures, computer paper, magazines, or even colorful junk mail.

If it's free, it's for me: Always ask for boxes when shopping at stores that still give away boxes. If the store offers free gift wrapping, let them wrap your packages as you finish shopping.

More freebies: Collect free sample products throughout the year and add one as decoration with a bow or instead of a bow when gift wrapping. For example, add a sample baby powder or baby oil bottle to a baby gift, or add a sample of any type of cosmetic to a teenage girl's gift.

On Christmas day don't throw away the crumpled-up wrapping paper. It's the perfect weight and thickness for packing up the ornaments and decorations for next year.

Spiced Centerpiece

For a beautiful and inexpensive holiday centerpiece, make a basket of scented pinecones. All you need is a basket, ribbon, pinecones, spray paint, glue, and cinnamon or ground cloves. Spray-paint the basket green or red and tie a matching bow around it. Either spray-paint the pinecones gold or silver or leave them their natural color. Using a cotton swab, dab the inside edges of the pinecone with clear-drying glue. Sprinkle with cinnamon or ground cloves. Tap off the excess spice and let dry. Arrange the pinecones in the basket. These baskets make nice hostess gifts. Make a few extra to keep on hand. The spice scent will last a long time.

O Christmas Tree

In the long run an artificial tree will be less expensive, but for some people the holidays just wouldn't seem right without a real Christmas tree. The price of trees has remained constant over the last several years.

You can get the best price and the freshest tree if you buy it directly from a Christmas tree farm. If you don't live near a Christmas tree farm, check prices at several roadside lots to make sure prices are competitive.

Choose a pine tree. They tend to be about ten percent cheaper than fir trees.

At many tree lots you can haggle on the price and get a few dollars knocked off. Of course the closer you wait until Christmas, the lower the price will be. By Christmas Eve the tree vendors will be out of business, and the few trees left are free to the general public. If you plan to put your tree in a corner or against a wall, look for a tree with a bad side and negotiate a low price on it. If you place the ugly side against the wall, it won't show.

Real Christmas trees are an all-American product, grown in all 50 states. Don't think you are contributing to the destruction of forests when you buy a cut Christmas tree. For every Christmas tree that is harvested, two to three seedlings are planted. According to the National Christmas Tree Association, about 1,000,000 acres are in production for growing Christmas trees.

Christmas Clay Ornaments

Make your own inexpensive Christmas ornaments out of clay. This is a fun project that will entertain your children or grandchildren during the Christmas holidays.

½ cup table salt
½ cup hot water
½ cup cold water
½ cup cornstarch
Food coloring if desired

Mix the salt and hot water in a large pan and bring to a boil. Place the cold water in a small bowl and stir in the cornstarch. Add the food coloring to the cornstarch mixture if desired. Add the cornstarch mixture to the boiling salt water and stir continually to keep the mixture from forming lumps. Cook over low heat until the mixture is stiff. Remove from heat and allow to cool slightly. Before it is completely cool, turn the mixture onto a cutting board. Let cool and knead until it is the consistency of clay. Store in an airtight container if you are not going to use immediately. To make Christmas decorations, roll out the dough and cut with cookie cutters or shape freehand. Use a toothpick or drinking straw to make a hole in the top for hanging. Bake at 200 degrees for 2 hours. Decorate and hang with string or twist ties.

December 26th

You can save a bundle next holiday season buying leftover holiday merchandise. Look for these bargains after Christmas; stock up and save.

Artificial Christmas trees fully decorated. Ask the store manager to hold one of the display trees for you until after Christmas. You should get the tree at 50 to

80 percent off the retail price of the tree and decorations. Be sure to ask for the box that the tree came in.

Chocolate for baking. Buy marked-down Christmas chocolate (packages of foil-wrapped holiday shapes) and freeze to use later in cookies, cakes, and all your baking. Chip the chocolate into pieces to make delicious chocolate chunk cookies. Use a vegetable peeler to make elegant chocolate shavings.

Butter cookies in tins. Drugstores and grocery stores will usually have tins of Christmas cookies left over. You can buy them for 50 to 80 percent off. Put the tins in the freezer and use throughout the year for lunchbox treats and snacks. Save the tins to fill with homemade goodies next year.

Plastic forks, knives, spoons, paper plates, cups and napkins. So what if they're red or green? Buy a one-year supply at 50 percent off or more. Use them all year long for picnics or parties and in lunchboxes.

Disposable tablecloths. Pick up a few in holiday patterns to wrap large packages with next year. They can be much cheaper than wrapping paper and are easier to work with.

Boxed Christmas cards for next year.

Turkeys and hams are always bargain priced during the holidays. Buy and freeze an extra turkey or ham to enjoy several months later. For best quality, ham that is not canned can be frozen whole or in slices for one month. Turkeys can be frozen for up to one year.

Special packages of beauty products that were holiday gift items. Department and drugstores will mark them down to giveaway prices to clear them out. You can usually find eye shadows, lipsticks, perfumes, nail polish, and other assorted beauty products.

SPRING

Fresh breezes motivate us to start cleaning the house. Use "home-brew" formulas instead of packaged cleaning supplies and save a bundle. And when you clean out your closets, turn your discards into cash. Springtime is also the time to start a garden. You can lower your grocery bill and eat better at the same time by growing your own fruits and vegetables. You don't have to be a homeowner to grow your own food. With container gardening, you can grow more than you might think on a small patio. Spring into savings!

SPRINGTIME MEANS CLEAN TIME

If you look under the kitchen sink in almost any house, you'll find a small fortune in cleaning supplies. Go to the bathroom and you'll find more of the same. Grocery and discount stores have several aisles dedicated to cleaning supplies. You can find a special high-priced cleaning product for just about any cleaning job. To save money on cleaning supplies, you have two good options—concentrates and home brews.

A Little Goes a Long Way

You can buy concentrated cleaning supplies from a janitorial supplier. Look in your telephone book under "janitorial supplies" for one near you. Most will sell directly to the public. Concentrated commercial products save money because they are less expensive than cleaning products sold at the grocery store or discount drugstore. They save time because they generally work faster and better and last longer. You'll also have lots of room under the sink, because they come in small packets.

To get started, you'll need to buy a few reusable plastic spray bottles to mix the concentrates in. Dilute the cleaners according to the directions on the concentrate packages. Don't fall into the assumption that if a little works well, a lot will work better. These products are formulated to work the best when the correct amount of water is added. Mixing the concentrates is easy; most packets are the right size for the spray bottles, so you don't even have to measure.

When mixing cleaners up from concentrates, add water to the bottle before pouring in the concentrate packet. This will keep the product from making tons of foam. After adding the packet, screw on the top and shake to mix the ingredients.

Home Brews

Very few cleaning jobs around the house cannot be handled with baking soda, vinegar, or ammonia. Buy all three in the largest or most economical size to use for cleaning. Try some of these home-brew cleaning formulas. They are easy to make and very inexpensive. Always label the bottle to show the contents.

Window Cleaner

1 pint water
½ cup rubbing alcohol
1 tablespoon ammonia
2 drops of blue food coloring (optional)

Pour into an empty spray bottle. This formula will clean windows effectively without streaking.

All-Purpose Cleaner

1 tablespoon liquid dishwashing soap
1 cup clear ammonia

Pour the dishwashing soap into a small spray bottle and add ammonia. Use it for cleaning the range top, counters, appliances, and just about anything else!

Toilet Cleaner

1 cup baking soda
1 cup powdered laundry detergent

Mix baking soda with powdered laundry detergent and store in a glass jar or plastic container. Sprinkle one-fourth cup into the toilet. Let it soak for a few minutes; swish it around with a toilet brush; let it soak for a few more minutes before flushing.

Alcohol works wonders at dissolving grease or removing ink and other stains. For best results, buy a bottle of pure alcohol (91 percent) at the drugstore and use it instead of clear drinking alcohol or rubbing alcohol.

Disinfectant

½ cup borax
1 gallon warm water

To make your own disinfectant cleaner, simply add ½ cup borax to one gallon of warm water. Use this to clean and disinfect the bathroom floors, the outside of the toilet, the tub, and ceramic tile walls. It does a great job at a very low cost.

Drain cleaner

¼ cup baking soda
½ cup vinegar

To help prevent grease buildup in your drains and to keep your drains smelling fresh, pour ¼ cup baking soda down the drain. Add ½ cup vinegar. Cover the drain tightly for a few minutes, then flush with cold water.

Furniture polish

¼ cup lemon juice (fresh or bottled)
½ cup olive or vegetable oil

To make home-brew furniture polish, mix lemon juice with oil. Store the homemade polish in a clean plastic or glass bottle. Use an old cotton rag to polish your wood furniture. Simply rub in a small amount of the polish. It will clean your wood furniture and make it shine.

To save the same rag to use each week just for dusting, place it in a plastic bag and close the top. You will have to add only a very small amount of furniture polish each week, since the rag will stay moist.

Wall Cleaner

This is a great formula for removing grease from painted walls in the kitchen.

¼ cup baking soda or borax
½ cup white vinegar
1 cup ammonia
1 gallon warm water

Combine ingredients in a bucket. Always wash walls from the bottom up, since dirty water dripping down the wall can leave streaks that are nearly impossible to remove.

Kitchen Cleanup Costs

Buy the cheapest liquid dishwashing detergent that you can find, but add a few tablespoons of vinegar to the dishwater. The vinegar cuts the grease and leaves the dishes sparkling clean.

Cut steel wool pads in half with kitchen scissors before using them. The smaller pads are easier to use, and your box will last twice as long. Steel wool pads won't get rusty if you store them in a plastic bag in the freezer. You can also use a loofah sponge instead of buying steel wool pads. To make a large loofah sponge into manageable pieces to work with, cut it lengthwise, then cut each half into six or eight pieces. Loofah sponges are much gentler to the hands than steel wool and will not rust.

Instead of throwing away a sponge that has a stale odor, simply toss it in the dishwasher and wash it with the next load of dishes. It will come out clean and fresh-smelling. The hot water from the dishwasher will also kill any bacteria in the sponge, so it's a good idea to wash your sponges in the dishwasher often.

Keep a bottle of vinegar within easy reach. When your stove, countertops, walls, or anything else becomes spattered with grease, pour or spray about a quarter of a cup of vinegar on the surface and wipe with a clean, dry rag. Vinegar cuts the grease and leaves a nice shine.

When cleaning stainless steel countertops, ranges, or sinks, use club soda. You can buy a small bottle of generic or store-brand club soda for about 50 cents. It cleans like a charm and dries to a gleam without streaks or spots. And if club soda has gone flat, it still works to clean stainless steel.

Save More on Your Floor

Vinegar is also the best cleaner for linoleum or ceramic-tile floors. Add about half a cup of white vinegar to half a bucket of warm water. This solution works better than any store-bought floor-cleaning product. It will make your floors sparkle and shine, and the cost is minimal.

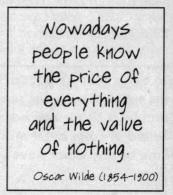

Nowadays people know the price of everything and the value of nothing.

Oscar Wilde (1854-1900)

Don't throw away odd socks or socks with holes in them. Use them to make a skinflint mop. Tie ten or 12 socks to a mop or broom handle and use just as you would a regular mop. White cotton socks work best. By the time the "sock mop" wears out, you will probably have accumulated plenty more socks for making a new one.

Q. How can I remove scuff marks from vinyl floors without buying yet another cleaning product?

A. To remove black scuff marks on vinyl or linoleum floors, use regular white toothpaste. Rub the paste into the black mark and wipe it away with a damp cloth. If the scuff marks are especially tough, add a little baking soda to the toothpaste. The marks should come right off.

The Most-Used Room in the House

To make a practically free container for your toilet brush, cut the top half off a plastic gallon or half-gallon milk container. You can leave the handle on it to make it easy to carry from one bathroom to another.

Instead of buying expensive lime removers for the toilet and other bathroom fixtures, try hydrogen per-oxide first. It can do the job for a fraction of the price.

To clean really stubborn hard water rings in the toilet bowl, pour some cola into the bowl and let it sit for one hour. You can use any brand of cola, but it must be cola, not lemon-lime or any other flavor. Flat cola works just fine.

To get nasty soap scum and dirt off your tub or shower, mix one part baby oil to four parts water in a spray bottle. Spray the mixture on a section and wipe off with a sponge. You won't find a cleaner at any price that gets soap scum off more easily. When you're done, just go over the area once with a disinfectant cleaner to make sure all the germs are killed.

Instead of buying expensive mildew remover, try using rubbing alcohol. It works well at removing mildew and other stains from the silicone caulking around the tub and any other areas where mildew forms.

For really tough jobs such as cleaning ceramic tiles, radiators, air vents, or dirty shower stalls, use ¼ cup baking soda in a gallon of very warm water with ½ cup vinegar and 1 cup clear ammonia. Wear rubber gloves and clean in a well-ventilated area.

You don't need to keep replacing plastic shower curtain liners because they are too hard to clean. The easiest way to get a plastic shower curtain liner really clean is to wash it in the washing machine. Fill the washing machine with warm water and two or three dirty towels (we all have plenty). Add ½ cup of laundry detergent and ½ cup of baking soda. Then wash, adding 1 cup white vinegar to the rinse cycle. Pull the shower curtain out after the rinse cycle, then let the towels continue through the spin-dry cycle. Hang up the shower curtain immediately. The wrinkles will disappear as the curtain dries. This is so easy that you won't be tempted to throw the shower curtain liner away when it gets dirty.

Soap Solutions

To keep your soap bars from melting into a soggy mess, place a sponge under each bar of soap. Use the soapy sponge to wash with. Not only does this help keep the area neat, but you will actually use most of the melted soap instead of washing the soapy mess down the drain. You'll find that your soap lasts longer.

Instead of throwing away the end pieces of soap, make soap on a rope by placing the small pieces inside an old pair of pantyhose.

When the bar of soap gets too small to handle, don't throw it away. You can make it into inexpensive soft soap for filling hand-soap dispensers. You can either melt the soap in hot water or blend the soap pieces in the blender with warm water to make soft soap.

Open bars of soap as soon as you buy them. They will harden and last longer. Place them in drawers to make your clothes smell fresh.

> Most families can afford to be without the wonderful household necessities no family can afford to be without.
>
> Anonymous

Instead of buying expensive liquid soaps for washing hands, fill your pump dispensers with the least expensive shampoo you can find. It works great and is very gentle to your hands.

Most household detergents are highly concentrated. Experiment with your favorite brand. You can usually use one-half to three-fourths of the suggested amount and still do the job right.

Scouring powder is often wasted because the containers have too many or too large holes. To keep the cleanser from coming out too fast, cover half of the holes with masking tape. You will find that you use less cleanser to do the job. This works especially well for when the children clean their own bathrooms!

Cleaning All Around the House

Use a plastic wastebasket as a scrub pail. The wastebasket gets washed out without any extra effort, and you don't have to spend money on an extra plastic bucket.

When washing windows, use old newspapers, pantyhose, rags, or socks instead of paper towels. These choices are inexpensive and won't leave lint on the windows.

Here's an easy, inexpensive way to clean upholstered furniture. Use a solution of ¼ cup of liquid dishwashing detergent and 1 cup warm water. Whip the solution into a high foam with an eggbeater. Apply the foam to the upholstery with a stiff brush, working on a small area at a time. Use a damp sponge to remove any soap residue. To speed drying time, use an electric fan.

Freshen the Air

Instead of buying expensive air fresheners, spray a little of your favorite perfume on a cotton ball and wipe it on lightbulbs around the house. When you turn lights on, the heat releases the scent.

Use plastic film canisters to make small air fresheners. Fill the canister with baking soda and poke a few holes in the lid. These air fresheners are perfect in drawers, cabinets, luggage, and trash cans. Replace the baking soda as needed.

Here's an easy way to make your own low-cost room air freshener. Just cut an orange, grapefruit, lemon, or lime in half, remove the pulp, and then fill the shell with salt. This skinflint air freshener will provide a pleasant aromatic scent anywhere in your home. Keep one under the kitchen and bathroom sinks. They really do work wonders! When you make fresh juice, save the rinds in the freezer until you need to make a new air freshener.

SPRING BEST BUYS CALENDAR

March

Apples, artichokes, beef, broccoli, chicken, eggs, fish, grapefruit, lamb, oranges, pineapple, scallops, turnips, coats, appliances, china, glassware, ski equipment, storm windows, hosiery, luggage, children's shoes, children's clothing.

April

Artichokes, asparagus, broccoli, chicken, eggs, fish, grapefruit, lamb, lemons, pineapple, pork, rhubarb, summer squash, turkey, dresses, hats, men's suits, patio furniture, air conditioners, shoes, vacuum cleaners, Easter candy, infants' wear.

May

Asparagus, beans, beef, broccoli, corn, cucumbers, eggs, fish, lamb, lemons, peas, pineapple, pork, rhubarb, strawberries, summer squash, tomatoes, tires, snow tires, lingerie, summer clothes, handbags, housewares, boys' clothing, men's clothing, blankets, bathrobes, TV sets.

A GREEN THUMB

A backyard garden is a frugal person's dream come true. It's almost like getting free food. With just a little money and a little work, you can have an abundance of fresh, healthful, delicious food. A vegetable garden can generate a steady supply of vegetables from spring to fall. It's not necessary to have a large garden to save money. Start small and work your way into it. Gardening is a fun hobby, and unlike other hobbies, instead of costing you money, this hobby will save you money. To get the most from your garden, try some of these tips and ideas.

If your time and space are limited, concentrate on growing foods your family likes, that are easy to grow, and that are expensive to buy in the grocery store. A good list to start with might contain tomatoes, green peppers, broccoli, lettuce, radishes, green beans, strawberries, and raspberries.

You'll need a few garden tools—a shovel, a hoe, a rake, and a trowel. But don't spend all your savings buying tools and gadgets. Garden stores and catalogs are full of gadgets and supplies that won't improve your yield or reduce your labor. The basics will get the job done. Shop garage sales and flea markets for used garden tools. A good tool will last a lifetime.

Before buying topsoil, check with your local county extension agent and see if any free soil is available in your area. You may also be able to get all the free wood chips and mulch that you can use for landscaping. You'll need a truck to take home the soil or mulch, but you can't beat the price!

Plant the same vegetable several times, perhaps at weekly intervals. This will assure you fresh vegetables over a longer period of time.

Weeds rob your plants of water and nutrients, so weed often. You can keep weeds away by covering the ground with a three-inch layer of hay or leaves. The hay or leaves also help keep moisture in the soil.

Use plastic gallon milk or water jugs to drip-irrigate thirsty crops like tomatoes or cucumbers. Simply poke a few holes in the bottom and sink the jug up to its neck in the middle of the bed. Fill the jug with water. The water will seep through the ground to thirsty roots, and not a drop will be lost to evaporation. You'll use less water and get better results. Plant jugs between the rows, spacing them a couple of feet apart.

> *It is thrifty to prepare today for the wants of tomorrow.*
>
> The Ant and the Grasshopper

Use old pantyhose to tie up tomato plants; it won't cut into the delicate vines. This is a low-cost solution compared with buying tomato cages.

Make a low-cost drip irrigation system for your garden out of an old leaky garden hose. Poke more holes in the hose with an ice pick or nail. Then lay the hose between the rows in your garden. Turn the water on low so that it will slowly drip out through the holes into the ground.

If you have problems with deer, rabbits, and other animals eating vegetables out of your garden, save some hair clippings or ask your barber or beautician to save some for you. Spread the hair clippings around the outside edges of your garden or flower bed. The animals will stay away from your vegetables or flowers.

Q. The seed packets always have too many seeds. How can I save extra seeds for next year?

A. Seeds need to remain dry; if they get wet, they will sprout. The best way to keep vegetable or flower seeds dry and organized is to store them in little bottles (baby food bottles are perfect) or plastic margarine containers that have a tight lid. Simply place the extra seeds into the clean, dry bottle or container and add a few tablespoons of flour or cornmeal to the container. The flour or cornmeal helps keep the seeds dry. Put the containers in a cool, dark place until you are ready to plant again. You can tape a picture from the seed packet on the outside of the container so you will know what seeds are inside. If the jar is clear, just fold the seed package and place it inside.

A Heap of Savings

Instead of paying to have kitchen scraps, leaves, and grass trimmings hauled off, build a compost heap. You'll end up with the best fertilizer around for your garden.

Compost is a dark, easily crumbled substance that develops from the partial decay of organic material. Making compost cuts down on garden refuse by reusing leaves, weeds, and grass clippings. The compost provides a mulching material for your plants and contributes organic material to your garden's soil.

One of the easiest and cheapest ways to make compost is in a compost heap. Start the compost heap directly on the ground. Begin with any plant material— vegetable peelings and scraps, grass clippings, garden prunings, leaves, hay, spent plants, straw, or weeds. Make this initial layer six to eight inches deep. Moisten the layer and add one to two inches of manure or one cup of commercial fertilizer. Add a layer of one to two inches of dirt on top of the compost pile.

Do not compost meat scraps or diseased vegetables. If you want, you can keep the compost pile in place with sides of wire, wood, or concrete block. Repeat the same layers until the compost pile is at least four feet deep. The compost pile will require six to twelve months before it is dark brown or black, crumbly, and ready to use. Turning the pile so the inside is moved to the outside and vice versa every four to ten weeks will speed up the composting process somewhat.

You can also work organic material—kitchen scraps, leaves, manure, and so forth—directly into the soil. Simply spread a two-inch to four-inch layer of a material such as leaves or vegetable peelings over the soil and work it in. Do this in the fall so the material has a chance to decay before planting.

The ABC's of Container Gardening

The high cost of food makes gardening very appealing. But if you think you can't reduce your grocery bill because you live in an apartment or condominium, think again. The answer to your problem is container gardening, and it's easier than you think. You can grow an abundant crop of fresh vegetables with just a few flowerpots on a sunny patio. Here's what you need to know to get started.

In most parts of the United States, you can plant anytime from the first of May until the first fall frost. If you live in a warm climate, you may be able to have a year-round harvest.

To get started, fill a couple of large pots with commercial potting soil. It's better to go ahead and spend the money on potting soil instead of using dirt, because potting soil has a lighter texture that allows roots to develop more efficiently. In addition, store-bought soil shouldn't harbor any insects.

Use any type of large pots you have around the house. Even plastic buckets work fine, once you cut a few holes in the bottom for drainage. If you don't have any pots you can spare, buy large black plastic disposable pots at a local nursery. The nursery buys these pots in bulk and probably will sell you several pots for less than a dollar each. If you are buying other supplies, the salesperson may even give you a few used pots.

Cheap plastic pots actually are better than expensive clay pots, because they tend to keep the soil moist longer. You'll need to water less frequently, which will help keep your water bill under control.

You can plant almost any type of vegetable in a container, but the best choices include tomatoes, squash, cucumbers, eggplant, and peppers. Place pots in a sunny location. Most vegetables need about six hours of sun every day. Water regularly, but wait until the soil is dry on top before watering again.

With container gardening you can expect a good harvest. Your container garden's yield should be almost the same as the yield of the same number of plants in a backyard garden. You don't have to be a homeowner to reduce your grocery bill with home-grown produce.

Houseplants

Don't waste money on special "grow lights" for indoor plants. Ordinary white fluorescent lights are cheaper, last longer, and work just as well.

Save water and save plants by knowing when to water them. Stick a pencil down into the dirt (be careful to avoid roots) in the flowerpot. If it comes out with dirt clinging to it, don't water. If it comes out dry and smooth, the plant needs a drink.

A GREEN THUMB

After cooking vegetables in water, by boiling or steaming, cool the water to room temperature and use it to water your houseplants. Your plants will slurp up the vitamins! It's like getting a free fertilizer.

Small flowering houseplants such as African violets, begonias, and bulbs (hyacinths, narcissus, or tulips) make lovely centerpieces. They not only cost less but also last longer than fresh-cut flowers.

FREE PLANTS

You can produce free houseplants by growing fruits and vegetables. The top of a pineapple makes an attractive plant. Remove the fruit and a few of the bottom leaves. Place the stem in an inch or two of water for a couple of weeks. Once it grows roots, you can plant it in a pot.

Stick three toothpicks into the large end of an avocado pit so that the picks are perpendicular to the sides. The toothpicks will hold the pit upright in a glass or jar by resting on the rim. Fill the jar with water so that the bottom of the pit is wet. Maintain that water level over a period of five or six weeks. When the pit develops a good root structure and has sprouted, plant the avocado in soil. Some avocado plants have grown into small trees.

A sweet potato makes a very attractive plant. If you have one that is getting soft, keep it in a brown paper bag until it sprouts and grows roots, then plant it in soil. The foliage is particularly appealing.

EGG ECONOMICS

Eggs are very versatile and economical. For those who are not on a low-cholesterol diet, eggs can be used in an almost unlimited number of ways for breakfast, lunch, dinner, or snacks. Eggs offer a large amount of protein for a small amount of money. They are one of the few foods that, without adding any other ingredient, can be made into a nutritional low-cost main course.

Egg grades and sizes determine the price of eggs. Most supermarkets carry Grade AA and A eggs. Some stores will even carry Grade B eggs. All the grades have the same nutritional value; the only difference is appearance. Grade B eggs usually have a thinner white and a flatter yolk. Regardless of the size of the egg, AA and A grades are perfect for poaching, frying, and cooking in the shell and, of course, are the highest-priced. Grade B eggs are less expensive and are a smart buy for baking, scrambling, making omelets, or use in any recipe when perfect appearance doesn't matter.

When checking the prices of eggs of the same grade but different sizes, keep this formula in mind: If the difference in the price per dozen between medium and large eggs of the same grade is 7 cents or more, the medium eggs are the better buy per pound. If the difference is 6 cents or less, the large eggs are the better buy per pound.

When you buy eggs for baking and cooking in recipes, you'll usually get more for your money if you buy medium eggs rather than large. Only rarely will you have to add an extra egg to a recipe to make up for size. Small eggs are not recommended for using in recipes.

To get the most for your money when you are buying eggs, you'll need to calculate the cost per ounce.

> *Enough is as good as a feast.*
>
> John Heywood
> (1497-1580)

For eggs to qualify as jumbo, a dozen eggs must weigh at least 30 ounces; extra-large eggs must weigh at least 27 ounces per dozen; large eggs must weigh at least 24 ounces per dozen; medium eggs must weigh at least 21 ounces per dozen; small eggs must weigh at least 18 ounces per dozen. To calculate the price per ounce, divide the retail price by the number of ounces per dozen.

Egg-citing Egg Facts

Eggs can be frozen, but not in their shells, which would crack. To freeze eggs, remove them from their shells and scramble them with 1 teaspoon salt or 1 teaspoon honey for each cup (about five eggs) to stabilize the yolks and keep them from getting pasty after thawing.

You can tell whether an egg is fresh by placing it in a pan of water. A fresh egg sinks to the bottom. An old egg floats, because the egg shrinks as it gets old and the extra space inside the shell is filled with air.

Always buy eggs from a refrigerated egg case. Eggs bought at room temperature from a farm or farmer's market will spoil much faster. Every day an egg is stored at room temperature, it loses more quality than it would during a week of refrigeration.

To save an egg that cracks as you boil it, pour some salt directly on the crack and return it to the boiling water. The salt will help seal the crack and keep most of the egg white inside the shell.

EGG ECONOMICS

You don't need to buy an expensive egg-poaching machine to make perfectly round poached eggs; use an empty tuna can! Remove the top and bottom with a can opener. Drop the clean tuna can rim in a pan of boiling water and crack an egg into it. You will have a beautiful poached egg made easily and thriftily. Add a drop or two of vinegar to the boiling water to keep the egg whites from spreading.

To get the freshest eggs, look for a stamped date on the egg carton and choose the carton with a date closest to the day you buy them. The stamped date is the actual date the eggs were packaged. On some egg cartons, you may find a stamped code instead of the actual date. The code will be a number such as 32. The 32 means the eggs were packaged on the 32nd day of the year, which would translate into February 1st.

To keep eggs fresh longer, store them in the refrigerator in their original container. These containers help them stay colder in the refrigerator. One of the worst places to store eggs is in the refrigerator door. Every time the door is opened, the eggs will get a blast of warm air.

Eggs to the Rescue

The two-egg omelet is one of the easiest, thriftiest ways to use up any leftover meats, cheeses, and vegetables. Simply cut up leftovers into bite-sized pieces. Mix two eggs in a bowl with a fork until the whites and yolks are just blended. Heat about a tablespoon of margarine in a skillet over medium heat. When the margarine is melted, pour the egg mixture into the pan and spread about half a cup of the leftovers on top of the egg mixture. Cook for about two minutes over medium heat, then flip the omelet over and cook for one to two minutes more until eggs are done. A two-egg omelet will serve one adult or two small children. Double or triple the recipe if you have lots of leftovers and you want to make this a one-course meal.

Q. Why do brown eggs cost more than regular white eggs? Are they better quality eggs?

A. There is no difference in taste or quality between brown eggs and white eggs. Brown eggs are laid by hens descended from Rhode Island Reds. They are larger birds that eat more feed, which produces higher prices for the eggs. Why pay more for brown shells, since it's the inside that you eat?

Easter Egg Decorating on a Shoestring

Decorated Easter eggs are a fun tradition that does not have to cost a bundle. You can save money by using a few fun and easy tips for decorating eggs the skinflint way.

For the best results, use only fresh, clean, unbroken eggs. The eggs should be hard-cooked and chilled before dyeing. Remove eggs from the refrigerator at least a half hour before cooking, since very cold eggs may crack when you put them in hot water.

You don't have to use an egg-dyeing kit that costs $2 to $4 for four colors. Easter eggs can be dyed with unsweetened powdered soft drink mix, which costs 10 or 20 cents per package. Just mix one package of drink mix with ⅔ cup of warm water. Drop the eggs into the mixture for about a minute. It's quick, easy, and inexpensive.

To make beautiful decorated Easter eggs without spending much money, gather some small leaves and flowers. Lay a few tiny flowers or leaves flat against an uncolored egg. Wrap the egg in a piece of old pantyhose material. Tie pantyhose closed around each end of the egg with string. Lower the egg into dye. Let the egg dry inside the pantyhose, then cut the fabric away. You will have a beautiful patterned egg. You can also use the leaves of fresh herbs such as parsley, rosemary, or thyme. Herbs make interesting prints on the eggs.

You can create an unusual pattern on the egg with this method. Just lay a paper towel over a piece of aluminum foil. Drop 8 to 10 drops of food coloring on the towel. Gently wrap the foil around the damp egg. Open and allow the egg to dry. You can use one or more colors on each egg.

Instead of buying the plastic green grass for Easter baskets, shred colorful paper or even newspaper to go into the bottom of the baskets.

Buy Easter baskets once and reuse them year after year. Pack them up in a box to save for next year.

Always fill Easter baskets with treats you make yourself instead of buying them premade. You'll get much more for your money.

If you make more colored eggs than your family will eat as boiled eggs, make egg salad or deviled eggs out of the colored eggs.

FABULOUS FREEBIES

What could possibly be better than a great bargain? How about something for free? Here are some useful freebies that can save you money. Check out the list and start collecting them!

Call your local pest control company for a **free termite inspection.** Think of the peace of mind you'll enjoy if they find you don't have termites. The pest control company will give you a free estimate for an extermination if you do. Note that this free service does not apply to the termite inspection needed for selling a house.

Ask your doctor for **free samples of prescription drugs.** If your doctor is thinking of a certain prescription for you, a sample will ensure the drug will work for you before you spend big money on an entire bottle.

Write your favorite food companies or call their toll-free number. Tell them how much you like their products and ask for **free recipes and coupons.** Also write polite letters of criticism to a company if you have a complaint. Most companies are oriented toward customer service and will usually replace an item or send you a refund if you are not satisfied. Speak up!

Check with your favorite do-it-yourself store for **free home improvement classes or demonstrations.** Also check with craft stores, fabric or sewing machine stores, or computer stores for free classes.

If you have time to spare, volunteer to be bumped from an overbooked airline flight to get a **free round-trip airline ticket.** Airlines have different policies, but most offer a free round-trip ticket to anywhere in the continental United States if you give up your seat.

Need free entertainment for a group of children? Many large fast-food and pizza chains offer **free tours**

for groups of children. Most not only give a very educational and interesting tour, but they also will usually give the children some sort of freebie such as a coloring book or food item.

Walk-in medical clinics offer a wide range of free services from time to time. Some of the most popular freebies are **cholesterol screening, vision testing,** and **blood pressure testing.** Call to find out when they will be offering the free services.

Hospitals offer many **free lectures** on various health topics. Call your local hospital for a schedule. Some even offer **free exercise classes** and **free diet and nutrition counseling.**

Most electric companies offer a **free energy audit**. Many will even install water-saving shower heads and other energy-saving devices at no charge. Be sure to ask about energy credits that can lower your utility bill every month.

The Internal Revenue Service has many **free information booklets** to help with your tax preparation and planning. Call 1-800-829-3676 for the booklet called "Guide to Free Tax Services."

Are you buried under a mound of debts? **Free credit counseling** and advice could be just a phone call away. Look in your yellow pages for a nonprofit consumer credit counseling service. Take a step away from owing money and toward saving money.

Adopt a **free pet** from your local pound or animal shelter. Usually the animal will already be neutered or spayed. If you are looking for a particular breed, ask the shelter to call you when they receive one.

Have you ever wondered how much money you will be entitled to when you reach retirement age? Call the Social Security Administration at 1-800-772-1213 and ask for a **free Personal Earning and Benefit Estimate**

FABULOUS FREEBIES

Statement to be sent to you; it can be a real eye-opener. You should check your file every three years to make sure all your earnings are being credited to your account.

Go to the cosmetic counters of department stores for a **free makeover.** They will show you how to apply makeup and give you some makeup tips for your specific skin type and coloring. They may even have some samples that you can take home to try.

Before traveling, contact government tourism offices, local chambers of commerce, and state and national park headquarters for free vacation planning information. Ask for **free tour information** and discount offers from local hotels, restaurants, and attractions.

FREE PRESCRIPTION DRUGS

If you have a low income, you may be able to get free prescription medicines directly from the drug companies through the Pharmaceutical Manufacturers Association. Companies that belong to the association offer more than 65 different free drug programs for people with low incomes. Some patients qualify even with annual incomes up to $25,000. If you qualify, all you have to do to get your prescribed drugs is to have your doctor contact the association. The association helps thousands of people who cannot afford to pay for their required medicines. To get more information on the free drug programs, write to the Pharmaceutical Manufacturers Association at 1100 15th St. NW, Washington, DC 20005.

TURN YOUR TRASH INTO CASH!

Springtime, when most of us get motivated to do some major spring cleaning, is the perfect time to have a garage sale. When you and your family clean out the closets, drawers, and under the beds this year, save all that junk and turn it into cash. If you don't think a garage sale is worth your time, think again! With proper planning, you can easily make $500 in two days. If you have some old furniture or large appliances to sell, you can double or triple that amount. So get cleaning and start a collection of treasures to sell at your garage sale.

Garage Sale Tips

Search for garage-sale items in every room of the house. Don't forget to look in the attic, any crawl spaces, storage trunks, drawers, tool sheds, or any other area where your family stashes seldom-used items. Examine every item critically. If you haven't used it in the last few years, why not go ahead and get some money out of it?

When in doubt, DON'T THROW IT OUT! You will be surprised and amazed at what people will buy. If you come up with stuff that you think really is just junk, put it in a box and mark it 25 cents or 50 cents for each item. People love it when they think they are getting a bargain!

Plan to have your sale on Saturday and Sunday. Don't have your garage sale on a holiday weekend. The holiday will get all the extra money that week!

Advertise

A well-written newspaper advertisement can bring big results. If you have more than one newspaper in your area, look to see which has the most garage-sale listings and run your ad in that one. Garage-sale shoppers will go from one sale to another. Make your ad appealing by listing your good items: tools, sporting goods, electronic equipment, toys, baby items, patio furniture, bicycles, and microwaves and other appliances. These are sure-fire sellers that will attract people to your sale. Use a catchy title to attract shoppers to your sale.

Make lots of signs to direct people to your garage sale. If you make them sturdy, you can reuse them year after year. Yellow paper and black markers make the best signs. Always put your address on the sign.

Make It Sell

Make everything in your sale sparkle. Houseware items will sell quickly if they are sparkling clean. Wash any clothes for sale and be sure to hang them up.

If you have a lot of clothing to sell, make a dressing room in the garage out of an old shower curtain. For security reasons, do not let strangers into the house to try on clothes or use the bathroom.

Price the merchandise approximately 20 to 30 percent of the retail value. Charge the most you would pay at a garage sale, and remember that most people will make you an offer lower than what's on the price tag. Price each item to make sure it sells. If you price one item too high and the buyer knows it, he or she will think everything is priced too high. Use removable stickers, white address labels, or masking tape to price merchandise. Make signs for large items. Mark damaged goods "as is."

Offer to sell merchandise for neighbors for a commission of 20 to 25 percent. Have them price the items and tell you the lowest price they will accept.

TURN YOUR TRASH INTO CASH!

Save small boxes and different-size shopping bags to use to pack up sold merchandise.

Pick up plenty of $1 bills, a few $5 bills, and some quarters at the bank. Price merchandise in even quarters so you won't have to worry about dimes, nickels, and pennies.

The Day of the Sale

Have all your merchandise priced the night before so you can quickly set up on Saturday morning. Be ready as early as possible. Shoppers will arrive early on the first day of your sale. But make sure you don't don't sell all your good stuff to the early birds at give-away prices.

Give your garage sale a fun, partylike atmosphere. Decorate the yard with streamers, balloons, flags, or anything else that will draw attention to your house.

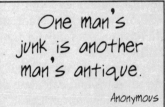

One man's junk is another man's antique.

Anonymous

If you have a television or radio for sale, have it plugged in and working. Let shoppers plug in any small appliances to make sure they work. You will get more money for your appliances and electrical items if shoppers are positive that they are in working condition.

The more items you have the better the sale will be. Spread your merchandise all over the yard if possible. Save old blankets or old shower curtain liners to put on the ground under the goodies.

Set up a refreshment stand and sell coffee, soft drinks, lemonade, popcorn, brownies, or cookies. This is a fun project for your children or grandchildren. Let older children collect the money and keep the profits.

Your shoppers will stay longer if they have something to munch on.

Always have extra lawn chairs on hand for people to sit on. When two or more people are shopping together, one shopper will not be rushed if the others are sitting down enjoying a cup of coffee or a snack. This will help increase your sales.

Handling the Money

Keep your money with you at all times. Cash boxes or cigar boxes full of cash are quick to disappear when not attended. Wear a fanny pack or keep your money in an apron pocket. Several times during the day, take most of the money into the house and lock it up.

Set up a checkout stand near the exit of your sale. It will let shoppers pay for their purchases as they head for their cars.

Keep a small calculator with you so you can quickly add up sales and calculate discounts when shoppers want to haggle on prices.

Accept only cash. Don't take any personal checks unless you know the person. Offer directions to the nearest automated teller machine if they seem serious about wanting to buy something.

Take a cooler with drinks, sandwiches, and snacks out to the garage with you to eat during the day. You can easily grab a bite between customers.

Never hold an item for someone unless they give you a nonrefundable deposit. People who say they don't have the money and need to run home and get their cash may not come back!

TURN YOUR TRASH INTO CASH!

If you have a truck or van, offer to deliver large items after the sale. If you get your asking price, you may even want to offer free local delivery. Of course you will put a "sold" sign on the item, but the good news is that people passing by will see the large item and stop to take a closer look at what you have for

TREASURE HUNTING

Shopping at garage sales is an excellent way to save money. You can find all sorts of low-cost treasures. Get the most for your money when you go garage-sale shopping by using these tips.

Get to the sale early—even a few minutes before the scheduled starting time. The good stuff goes fast, especially if it is bargain priced.

Ask questions about items you are interested in buying. Why are you selling it? How old is it?

When you find something you want to buy, make an offer. If the price seems high, offer half the asking price. If the price is more in line, offer about 75 percent of the asking price. Hold out the amount of cash you are willing to pay so the seller can see it. Sometimes seeing the cash makes the seller more likely to accept your offer.

If you plan on buying several items from the same sale, make them an offer for all the items. You should be able to get a bigger discount for buying more items.

If possible, drive a pickup truck, van, or station wagon when you go garage-sale shopping to help you bring large purchases home.

sale. This helps keep the good stuff at your sale longer to attract customers.

The End of the Sale

Be ready to mark down prices on the last day if you want to clear out the junk. If you are planning another garage sale soon, store away the items that did not sell. Chances are they will sell next time. If you are moving or just want to get rid of the stuff, make arrangements to donate leftover items to a charity. Get a receipt for tax purposes.

After the sale, pick up all the signs you posted and save them for the next sale. Think about what you are going to do with all the extra cash!

HEALTHY, WEALTHY, AND WISE

If you added up the costs of prescriptions, over-the-counter drugs, and other health-related items you buy, you'd probably be shocked at the total. But you can save money and not sacrifice on quality.

At the Drugstore

When treating yourself with an over-the-counter medication, always ask the pharmacist for advice. A pharmacist can advise you on the value and benefits of one product over another. He or she can also help you save money by recommending the right product and possibly a generic equivalent. A pharmacist can also explain the proper way to take the medication and make sure that the over-the-counter medication will not interfere with any prescription medications you take.

Don't pay extra for brand-name vitamins; you're just paying for advertising and more expensive packaging. Only a few companies actually make vitamins, and they supply all the companies that sell them under different names.

Use empty film canisters instead of those expensive pill reminders to keep track of daily doses of pills. Once a week fill seven empty canisters with each day's dosage for the coming week and mark it with the appropriate day. The film canisters work wonders in helping elderly family members remember to take their medications.

Exercise Your Right to Save

You don't have to pay hundreds of dollars to join an exclusive health club to get in shape. You can get plenty of exercise without spending plenty of money.

Check with local schools, hospitals, churches, or women's clubs for free or inexpensive exercise classes. You'll meet some new friends, get in shape, and save money at the same time!

Make your own inexpensive exercise video by setting the VCR to record aerobic or exercise shows on television. Find a show you like and tape several episodes. Then you can do a workout whenever you find the time. When you get tired of the routines you have taped, simply tape some more shows.

Q. I exercise a lot and seem to get more than my share of athlete's foot. I spend a small fortune on over-the-counter medications. What can I do to save money and reduce my chances of getting athlete's foot?

A. To avoid athlete's foot, wear cotton socks. If your feet perspire a great deal, before working out sprinkle cornstarch in your socks and shoes just like powder. If you shower at a gym, always wear shoes—beach shoes or thongs—to significantly reduce your chances of getting athlete's foot.

Hot and Cold First Aid

Freeze unpopped popcorn in small plastic bags to use for ice packs. It really works—no watery mess. When the popcorn is no longer cold, you can simply refreeze it and use it again.

Keep a wet sponge in the freezer for an emergency ice pack that is ready to go. Dampen the sponge and apply to the sore area. Or you can quickly grab a package of frozen vegetables (such as peas) to ice down a bump or bruise.

If you need a hot-water bottle quickly but can't find one, try this homemade solution. Pour hot (not boiling) water into an empty plastic soda bottle and wrap it in a towel. You'll find quick relief without having to spend money on a hot-water bottle.

Lower Health-Care Costs

If you live near a medical or dental school, you may be able to take advantage of health and dental services offered by the school as part of the students' training. The cost for these services will be very low, sometimes even free. The students are supervised, and you will get the advantages of the newest procedures and practices.

When you must stay in the hospital overnight, you can save money by bringing your own toiletries and other items. The hospital will be more than happy to provide you with razors, toothpaste, tissues, or other supplies, but the price will be staggering!

Check with your local health department for all sorts of free or low-cost services. They may offer anything from cholesterol screening to free or reduced-cost vaccinations and immunizations.

Always wear sun block! The money you spend on sun block will save you big money in lower health-care costs later in life. A tanned body may look good now, but the physical and financial costs of skin cancer are not worth it!

Even if your insurance pays your hospital and doctor bills, check the bills carefully for errors. If you find any discrepancies or questions, be sure to find out the answers. This is one way we all can help to control the skyrocketing costs of health care.

HOSPITAL EXPENSES

One hospital stay can totally wipe out your savings and throw a monkey wrench in your budget for many months or even years. Even with a comprehensive medical insurance policy, your out-of-pocket costs probably will be more than you expect.

If your hospital stay is a scheduled visit instead of an emergency, you can save yourself some money by setting up a game plan. Believe it or not, there are many different ways to negotiate and to make your hospital stay more pleasant.

Ask the Doctor

Most people are prepared to talk to their doctor about the most intimate details of their lives but are not prepared to talk about money. Although you may feel embarrassed to talk to your doctor about finances, even doctors say the subject should be discussed more openly. It's not necessary to blow the subject out of proportion. Simply asking about fees, especially if you are a new patient, alerts the doctor to your interest in keeping costs down and encourages the doctor to take a look at prices.

Get a Second Opinion

Before you have any surgery, you should and are probably required by your insurance company to get a second opinion. Do some detective work yourself by calling surgeons or doctors before you go for a second opinion. You can do a price comparison of your local area and find out if your doctor's price is in line. If the second opinion price is lower than the amount your doctor charges for the procedure, ask your doctor if he or she will match the price. Price is an important factor, but quality care is the most important factor. Don't automatically go with the low bid unless you feel extremely comfortable that the doctor is very qualified and competent.

Negotiate

Fees for medical services are negotiable (except for Medicare patients), and many times the cost is determined by who pays the bill. A doctor will be more likely to bill you at a higher rate if he or she knows your insurance company will pay it in full. If you are paying for it out of your pocket, he or she may be more willing to charge you less. One of the best ways to save money is to find out how much your insurance company will pay for a particular procedure and ask your doctor to accept that amount as full payment.

Whenever negotiating anything, be pleasant but persistent. You may have to make several phone calls and wait for a return phone call with an answer. Don't give up prematurely. If you get a "no" answer, ask to speak to the supervisor. The higher you go, the better your chance of success.

Your insurance company may have more leverage for giving you additional perks. For example, you may be able to negotiate a private room or in-home care after the surgery if you can convince the insurance company that these benefits will speed your recovery and save them money in the long run.

Know the Rules

Know your insurance company's policies to make sure you get fully reimbursed. If your hospital visit is planned surgery, your doctor will usually handle all the paperwork. But in case of an emergency, you need to know which hospital to go to. Most insurance companies require that you call and get an authorization number within a certain time frame, such as 24 hours. Going to the wrong hospital or failing to get an authorization number can cost you big bucks! Read the material your insurance company gives you and write notes to keep with your insurance card in case of an emergency.

Paying the Bill

After your hospital stay, ask your insurance company to reevaluate your doctor and hospital bills. Your insurance company may be able to get some of the charges drastically reduced. They can look for charges that were not authorized by them and therefore should not be on the bill.

Do not pay the hospital bill when you check out. The hospital is required to give you a normal billing cycle, which is usually 30 days, to pay your bill. Use this time to review the bill and check for any errors or duplicate charges.

Wait until after the insurance company pays its portion of the bill before you pay the balance due. Your insurance company may have the bill reduced. If your insurance company denies your claim or any part of your claim, you can appeal the decision.

Try for a Cash Discount

Once you get the bills from the doctors who treated you, keep in mind that most people stretch out their payments on these bills. Doctors and hospitals are very aware that their bills are typically the last ones to get paid. People pay their rent, utilities, and food before even thinking about the medical bills. Doctors and hospitals are forced to write off huge amounts of receivables that they cannot collect every year.

Because of this, you might be able to get a discount if you pay in full right away. If you can afford to do that, call the doctors and ask how much they will discount the bill. Sometimes they will discount up to 50 percent for cash. Usually they will tell you exactly how much to send in, and frequently they will give you a deadline. They may say something like, "Send in $455.93 by February 1, or the full balance will be due."

It is important to keep your promise, because they will not offer you another deal if you do not hold up your end of the bargain.

If money is very tight, make a payment every month to each of the doctors. Even a $5 payment should keep your account from being turned over to a collection agency. It is very important to tell the person in charge of accounts receivable that you can't afford to pay your portion of the bill in full. They will probably offer to discount your debt. What they want you to do is to borrow money from friends or relatives to pay off the bill. Whatever arrangements for payment you make with them, ask them to send you a summary of the new terms in writing. Be cooperative so they will be patient with you. If you avoid their calls, they will quickly turn your account over to a collection agency.

If you have been making monthly payments to the doctors and eventually have the money to pay off the full balance, call them and ask for a discount for pay-

> *It never fails: When it is most difficult to meet expenses, you meet them everywhere.*
>
> Anonymous

ing off the bill. Because sending out invoices and having collectors call every month are expensive, most are very eager to get your account cleared up. At this point they may offer you a discount. Ask them to tell you exactly how much is due to pay off the entire debt. When you make this final payment, include a letter stating who you talked to and that this final payment will bring your balance to zero.

After you have paid all your medical bills, get a copy of your credit report (see page 96). Many health-care providers will, as a matter of policy, put a negative comment on it if your bill is not paid in full right away. These negative comments will follow you for seven years if you do not get them cleaned up.

INSURANCE

One of the most overlooked sources for saving money is homeowner's insurance. Most families will comparison shop for their homeowner's policy just once, then blindly continue to pay the premiums each year. It's much easier to renew every year with the same carrier than to force yourself to go through the process of shopping your policy.

By taking a few hours to shop around for a new policy, or even just by reading the fine print of your current one, you can cut your home insurance bill by as much as 50 percent! Some homeowners qualify for various premium-slashing discounts without realizing it. Others stick with policies sold to them by insurance agents when they'd be better off eliminating the middle man and buying coverage from direct writers.

Direct Insurance Writers

Direct writers are very selective about who they will cover; your house has to meet their criteria for a very low-risk house. But if your house is accepted, it's almost a sure bet that the lowest quote will come from one of the direct writers. These companies have the lowest selling costs, and they can pass the savings on to you. The top direct writers are American Express (1-800-535-2001), Amica (1-800-242-6422), and USAA (1-800-531-8100).

National Companies

If the direct writers won't accept you, you'll need to try the big national companies. These companies pay an average commission of about 8 percent, so they can work up quotes that are nearly as low as the direct writers'.

Independent Agents

Only as a last resort should you work with an independent agent (one who represents many different companies). An insurance company that works through agents pays 12 to 21 percent in commissions. The agency writers simply can't be as competitive.

Ways to Save

Once you have settled on your carrier, it's time to work out the best deal. You can quickly knock hundreds of dollars off your annual policy by taking advantage of the many discounts that nearly every insurer offers. You can get discounts for burglar alarms; upgrading electrical, heating, or plumbing facilities; renovations; smoke alarms; sprinklers; burglar bars; and even having a live-in housekeeper. Discounts are available for new homes, nearly new homes, retirees, and "good" customers (those who have been with the company for many years without a claim).

One of the quickest ways to save big money on your homeowner's insurance is to raise your deductible (the amount you will pay when you have a claim before the insurance coverage starts). The standard deductible is $250, but some go as low as $100. Raising your deductible from $250 to $500 will save about 12 percent. If you go from $250 to $1,000, the savings will be approximately 24 percent. And if you can handle a deductible of $2,500, expect to save about 30 percent.

Another way you can save on homeowner's insurance is by belonging to a group that your insurance company deems "responsible." Several insurance companies offer discounts to university alumni and employees and other business clubs. To find out if any discounts are available, call your alumni association or business club to see if it has a special discount.

If your house is constructed of slow-burning materials such as brick or concrete, you can get a discount ranging from 5 percent to 15 percent. However, if more than one-third of the house is wood, you won't qualify for this discount.

You may be able to save money by insuring your cars and house with the same company. If you combine your homeowner's policy with your auto policy, many companies offer up to a 15 percent discount.

Before you automatically renew your homeowner's insurance this year, take a little time to do some research. With just a few phone calls, you may be able to cut quite a bit off your annual premiums.

Cut the Cost of Auto Insurance

Premiums are higher for cars that are frequently stolen or have high accident losses. It pays to make a phone call to your insurance carrier before driving the car off the lot.

Periodically shop around for the best rate. Your insurance company may have offered the best rate for you last year, but they will not necessarily have the lowest rate this year. One insurance company may charge double for exactly the same coverage. A few phone calls could save you big money.

If you already have health insurance and you are also paying an extra premium for medical coverage on your automobile policy, you are probably wasting your money. In most cases you can collect from only one policy, not both. Provided you have adequate health insurance coverage, canceling the medical portion of your auto insurance can shave 10 to 30 percent off your premiums.

Don't pay additional money to your insurance company for towing insurance if you are a member of an auto club that sends help in emergencies.

Ask About Discounts

Every company has a different set of discounts; some give discounts for cars equipped with air bags, automatic seat belts, anti-theft devices, and anti-lock brakes. Taking a defensive driving course can also earn you a discount from some insurance carriers. Nonsmokers may even qualify for a discount.

Increase your deductible. Changing your deductible from $200 to $500 for comprehensive and collision coverage can slash your insurance rate by 15 to 30 percent. Stash the saved money in a bank account so that you can easily come up with the deductible if you have to make a claim.

If you have an older car with a low replacement value, you can skip comprehensive and collision insurance. You don't have to be in an accident that completely wrecks your car to have it totaled. In many cases the insurance company will probably pay you the car's cash value rather than pay to repair it. When your car is around five years old, the insurance will quickly start to cost more than the amount of money the insurance company would pay if the car were totaled or stolen.

Insure all the cars in your household or immediate family with the same insurance company. You'll get additional discounts for each car that is added on the policy.

Be a safe driver. Drivers with a clean driving record—no traffic violations or accidents—for the last five years may be eligible for a discount. On the other hand, you'll pay additional premiums for each traffic violation, and insurers will add a surcharge for accidents that are your fault. A minor accident can add 10 to 15 percent to your premiums, and an alcohol-related accident can more than double your insurance—if they don't cancel your policy.

Insurance You Can Do Without

Some types of insurance coverage are so expensive for the amount of coverage you get that you can probably save money by skipping them.

Credit life insurance. Credit life insurance, which is offered to applicants for mortgages and car and boat loans, will pay off the loan if the borrower dies. It is supposed to give the borrower the peace of mind of knowing their survivor will not lose the house or car. Many people mistakenly assume they are required to buy this type of insurance in order to qualify for the loan. It is very expensive. A much cheaper way to safeguard the possession is to buy life insurance. Figure out how much money your spouse will need to pay off all existing bills, and buy a life insurance policy to cover this amount plus living expenses.

Private mortgage insurance (PMI). Unless you make a large down payment, you are usually required to buy PMI when you take out a home mortgage. The insurance is to protect the lender in case you default on the loan. After you have paid 20 percent of the original mortgage, you can drop the PMI and save $25 to $35 or more each month. Ask your mortgage company when you can qualify to drop the insurance. Your insurance company will not notify you that PMI can be dropped. If you don't ask to have PMI dropped, you will be charged the insurance for the entire life of your loan. It's just money down the drain!

Health insurance for cancer. Insurance for one particular disease or injury is popular right now because the policies are very profitable to the insurance companies. They sound appealing, but your comprehensive medical insurance should cover all medical problems.

> Many a man loses a lot of money through the hole in the top of his pocket.
>
> *Anonymous*

Life insurance for children. Start a college fund or savings account instead. Losing a child is an emotional drain on the family, not a huge financial drain, since children don't usually provide the family income.

Medical or baggage insurance for travelers. Your comprehensive medical insurance will cover you while traveling. Baggage insurance is automatically offered by the airlines. Even your homeowner's policy may pay for lost or stolen baggage.

Senior citizen burial cost insurance. These policies are expensive for the amount of money that is paid out. Funeral costs can be paid from the senior's life insurance policy instead.

Contact lens insurance. The insurance is usually just as expensive as replacement contact lenses!

Lost-credit-card insurance. These polices offer a hot line to call if your credit cards are lost or stolen. Make your own list of credit cards and numbers to call and keep it with your valuable papers. Save yourself the $25 to $75 per year.

INSURANCE

Pet insurance. The premiums on these policies are very expensive. Be sure to read the fine print if you sign up for one. Some offer comprehensive coverage, but many are so restrictive about what they cover that you are better off without the policy.

Rental car insurance. Call your insurance company before leaving for vacation; since most insurance companies cover you no matter what car you are driving, you do not need the coverage from the rental car agency. The additional insurance coverage can nearly double the cost of your rental car.

MORE THAN A READING ROOM

If you're looking for low-cost entertainment for the whole family, you can't beat your local library. If you live within the community, you usually can get a library card free. If you haven't been in the library recently, you'll be pleasantly surprised at all the different kinds of items you can check out and all the services the library offers. Although services vary from one library to another, you should be able to find plenty of free entertainment at your local library. Look at the calendar of events or the bulletin board for special activities and services.

Many libraries offer these money-saving services:

Books. Why buy a book, even a paperback, if you're going to read it only once? You can find best-sellers, mysteries, romances, and literature at the library. And if you think you might be interested in buying a particular book, checking it out of the library is a good way to preview it.

Cookbooks. You can find hundreds of cookbooks at the library. Instead of buying many cookbooks that may end up just sitting on a shelf, check them out of the library at no charge. Library books can usually be checked out for two or three weeks, which is plenty of time to try out a few new recipes. Make recipe cards of the best recipes that you find. Soon you'll have a recipe box full of the best recipes from a number of cookbooks.

Videos. The selection of videos varies from one library to another. Some libraries have just instructional and how-to videos, whereas others carry all types of videos including recent movies. Many libraries have an extensive collection of children's videos. The library may charge a $1 or $2 fee for taking out videos.

MORE THAN A READING ROOM

Books on tape. Cassette tapes of popular books are a hit with people who travel a lot by car, but they are expensive to buy. You can check the tapes out just like a book, and instead of listening to radio commercials on the way to work, you can listen to a book instead.

Meeting rooms. Need a meeting room? Check with your local library; they may have a meeting room that you can use. The rates will be low—in fact, if your organization or club is nonprofit, the library could be your ticket to a free meeting room.

More Services

Here are some additional services your library may provide:

Newspapers. Look for your local newspapers and other newspapers, such as *The New York Times,* from around the country.

Reference assistance. The reference department librarian can assist you in finding a reference book on almost any subject you are interested in. Children can find all the information needed for school book reports and projects, and adults can find books to help with work projects or a job search. Usually reference books cannot be checked out.

Typewriters, word processors, or computers. Need to type up a report? Many libraries have typewriters and computers that you can use.

Classes and lectures. Want to learn how to trace your family tree or balance your checkbook? Get a schedule of classes and special lectures offered at your local library. Most are free or very inexpensive and quite enlightening.

Newsletters. Look for all sorts of educational newsletters on everything from financial information to health, exercise, or cooking. Newsletter subscriptions can be very expensive—read newsletters in the library instead.

Photocopy machines. For pennies you can make a copy of an article or page that is of special interest to you.

Out-of-town phone books. Instead of paying for a long-distance directory assistance call, look up the number instead. Larger libraries have extensive phone book collections, and some even have all the information on computer.

Internet access. Some larger libraries have computers that are hooked up to the Internet to allow patrons to browse the World Wide Web.

CRAFTY SOLUTION

If you enjoy making crafts, look for books on your favorite crafts at the library. You'll find craft ideas and patterns that you can trace or copy for free. Before you buy another expensive pattern book for needlepoint, look to see what's available at the library.

For the Wee Ones

Let your child spend an afternoon at the library. The children's room might have fun services and scheduled events like these:

- Story hours
- Special films or movies
- Games and puzzles
- Reading contests
- Summer reading programs
- Magazines and comics

LET US ENTERTAIN YOU

Entertainment can be a drain on the budget. Use these strategies to make a night out more affordable. If you plan in advance, you can save quite a bit on movie and theater tickets.

Miserly Movies

Probably the cheapest way to watch a movie is to check out a video from the library. But not every library carries current films. Most of the time, renting movies at the video store is also cheaper than seeing the movie in the theater. Shop around for the best deal if you rent movies often. Prices vary from one video store to another. Some video rental stores offer discounts. On slow days such as Tuesday, you may be able to rent two videos for the price of one.

If you must see a movie at the theater, go early in the day. You can save up to 50 percent by attending a matinee show. Generally you can get a discounted movie ticket for afternoon movies and shows that start before 6 P.M.

If you are a senior citizen or a student, you may be eligible for discounted tickets to all shows. Ask before you buy your tickets. Students will need a student ID, and seniors will need a driver's license or other photo ID to prove their age.

Don't blow your savings at the concession stand. Food and drink prices are outrageous at the movie theater. Eat a snack or meal before or after the movie.

Thrifty Theater Tickets

In most major cities, you can get discounted theater tickets for same-day shows. While you probably won't be able to get discounted tickets for the most popular shows—they can be sold out months in advance—you should be able to enjoy an exciting evening without going broke. Call the tourist bureau in your city to find out where to buy discounted theater tickets.

Some repertory theater groups have "preview nights" before the play's regular run. The audience pays a discounted price for their tickets and participates with the company in a critique after the play.

If tickets to a special concert or local play are out of your price range, find out if you can attend a rehearsal. Attending the dress rehearsal the night before the show opens is almost as good as being there on opening night.

Season of Savings

If you love the theater, the symphony, or a local sports team and plan to attend every concert or game, you can save money buying season tickets. Season ticket holders usually get the best seats and tickets at reduced prices. If you just want to attend a few select concerts or games, look in the newspaper for personal ads from season ticket holders wanting to sell some of their tickets.

Cheap Concerts

Especially in the summertime, you may be able to find free concerts in your community. The talent at free concerts can range from "home grown" to top-notch and professional. Regardless, many free concerts are pleasant outdoor events in a local park.

PAMPERED PETS

We love our pets just as we do any other member of the family, and it's easy to get caught up into spending a bundle of money on them. But we can save money without Fido or Fluffy feeling any less loved.

To save money, adopt a pet from a local animal shelter instead of buying a pet from a pet store or a breeder. Some shelters offer free pets, but even if the shelter charges a small adoption fee (usually $25 to $30), you'll still save money. The same animal can cost several hundred dollars when purchased from a pet store or breeder. Many shelters offer reduced fees on basic veterinary care, and often shots and neutering or spaying are included in the adoption fee. If you are searching for a particular breed, ask the animal shelter if they will call you when one is available for adoption.

Frugal Feeding

To save money on dog or cat food, with your vet's permission, switch from canned food to dry food. When you buy wet food, you are paying extra for water and more packaging.

Feed your pet generic or store-brand food. You'll find that your pet is just as healthy and satisfied with a low-cost brand. The savings can add up to 25 to 50 percent or more.

Save money and preserve your pet's health by not overfeeding him or her. If you can't feel the ribs easily, reduce his or her food a little bit at each meal. Ask your veterinarian approximately how much your pet should weigh.

Resist the temptation to stock up on dry pet food. Even with proper storage, the vitamins and minerals in the food deteriorate after a few months, and the food could become moldy. Buy only the amount your pet will eat within a couple of weeks, even when it is on sale.

Save on Supplies

Instead of buying an expensive cat litter with a built-in deodorizer, buy an inexpensive brand of cat litter and add baking soda to the bottom of the litter box to absorb more odors.

Never buy dog collars. Instead go to garage sales, thrift stores, and flea markets; they always have low-priced belts. Buy a belt and cut it to the correct size and punch holes in it with an ice pick. It works just like a dog collar for a fraction of the cost.

Make an inexpensive cat scratching post by stapling a carpet remnant onto a log. You can then nail the log to a wooden base. Your cat will enjoy playing with this for hours, and maybe the furniture will be spared.

If your cat goes crazy for catnip, you can save money by growing your own. Catnip is easy to grow. One packet of seeds will harvest enough catnip for the year. You can expect to get three or more cuttings. Just dry the cuttings as you would fresh herbs. Tie off the toe end of an old sock and pour a little catnip into the sock. Tie the other end closed. Your kitty will be ecstatic.

Bargain Bathing

Bathe and groom your dog yourself. Some people pay more money to have their pets bathed and groomed than they spend on their own haircuts. You wouldn't pay to have your children's hair washed and combed, so why should you pay for your pet's baths?

REDUCE, RECYCLE, AND REUSE

Saving money and saving the environment easily go hand in hand. Each of us can do some simple things that not only save money, but also help save the environment.

If everyone used each disposable item at least twice, we'd cut our daily trash amount in half! Not to mention the cost savings. We'd save money by buying half as many disposable items, and we'd save in trash collection expenses.

Decrease unnecessary car trips by calling ahead to make sure the store has what you need before you jump in the car. Combine errands into one trip to conserve time and gasoline.

According to one estimate, one dollar of every $11 spent on groceries in the United States is spent on packaging. Shop for items by price and look for the most austere packaging. Buying loose vegetables should cost you less, since no packaging is required. You also can buy just the right amount for your family, thus eliminating waste. Look for concentrated items, such as juice and laundry products, that require less packaging and usually cost less, too.

Some products offer refill packages that save money and packaging. You can find everything from detergents to shampoos and lotions. Save the plastic bottle or box and fill it up with the cheaper refill package.

You can find more products made from recycled materials at the grocery and discount stores now. Napkins, trash bags, and paper towels are all available made from recycled materials. When these products were first introduced, they were the most expensive on the shelf. Many are now competitively priced, and some are even the best buys.

REDUCE, RECYCLE, AND REUSE

Instead of throwing items away, either sell them at your next garage sale or donate them to charity. If you sell them at the garage sale, you'll have some extra money; if you donate them to charity, someone else will use the item, and you'll have a tax deduction.

Landfills are clogged with lawn clippings because most people bag them up and throw them away.

> When your outgo exceeds your income, your upkeep is your downfall.
>
> Anonymous

Instead of bagging them, start a compost pile and use the compost around trees and in flower beds. You can layer dirt, grass clippings, and scraps and trimmings from the kitchen. See page 139 for directions.

Keep all household equipment in good repair. The longer an item lasts the more money you save.

Consider buying a used appliance or tool if it will do as well as a new one. You'll pay a fraction of the cost of a new model.

Rent or borrow seldom-used equipment. You can rent almost anything. If you plan to use it just once or twice, you'll be many dollars ahead by renting or borrowing.

Before you toss anything in the trash or place it in the recycling bin, ask yourself if you can use it for another purpose. The tubes from toilet paper rolls can keep extension cords tidy. Mesh onion bags can be wadded up and secured with a rubber band for a free scouring pad. Look at each item you throw out from another angle. You'll save money and reduce waste if you can use the item instead of buying another product.

SHOPPING SALE-A-BRATION

Everybody knows you can stretch a dollar by buying things on sale. But sales can be so seductive that you wind up buying things you don't need or can't use just because they're on sale. If you "save" 40 percent on an unnecessary item, you've really wasted 60 percent. Follow these guidelines to get the most out of your bargain shopping.

• Plan ahead and make a list of things you really need. Keep a notebook of sizes for all family members.

• Get to the sale early. The best bargains go quickly. Sometimes you can even slip in the night before a big sale, while the sales clerks are marking down the merchandise, for the best selection.

• Check the return policy for this particular sale. Even stores with generous return policies sometimes run sales for which you can't return merchandise. Knowing the return policy is especially important if you are buying something for a picky family member. No-return sales usually have the best markdowns and are the last sale of the season.

> Never buy what you do not want, because it is cheap; it will be dear to you.
>
> Thomas Jefferson
> (1743-1826)

• Don't buy any clothing that does not fit well. You're not going to miraculously wake up five pounds lighter in the morning. An item that does not fit well will just get pushed to the back of the closet.

• If the store sells out of an item you want, ask if a rain check is available. Rain checks are usually available for an advertised sale price, but not for clearance or special-purchase merchandise.

The No-fail Sale Test

Take this quick test to find out if a purchase really is a bargain.

1. Do you need it?

2. Is the item well made, a classic style, and in perfect condition?

3. If it is clothing, is it the correct size? Does it feel good on and make you look good?

4. Is the price at least 35 percent off the original price?

5. Can you afford to pay cash, or if you charge it, can you pay the bill right away?

If you can answer yes to all five questions, then you probably have a bargain. More than one no answer probably means you should pass on the deal.

SALE JARGON

On Sale generally means the item is discounted only temporarily. The sale may be advertised or unadvertised.

Clearance Sale generally means that the price has been significantly reduced to clear out merchandise. This happens typically at the end of the season.

Special Purchase doesn't really mean a sale price at all. The price is a lower regular price made possible because the store got a bargain on the purchase and wanted to pass the savings on to the customers.

APRIL 15

Income taxes are among our largest expenses, second only to housing for most American families. Depending on where you live and your income level, your income taxes will be 15 percent to 45 percent of your annual income. Most of it is money you never get to see. It is usually deducted from your paycheck before you ever get to touch it.

Despite this huge expense, for most people "tax planning" happens too late. The only time most people consider their taxes is at the time they fill out the annual return. Consequently, because of ignorance, many people pay more taxes than they are required to. Not knowing what tax breaks they are entitled to, people with average incomes end up overpaying their taxes because they feel they can't afford to hire a tax preparer. Here are some basic tax strategies that you can use to save money.

Educate yourself. One way to learn more about taxes is to take a continuing education course at your local community college on tax preparation. The tuition will be modest, maybe even free if you are over 55. The information will be up-to-date, and you can ask the teacher any questions you have. Even if you do not think you can complete your entire tax return yourself, you will learn some money-saving ideas relating to your particular circumstances to pass along to your tax preparer.

Try to break even. Getting a large tax refund each year might seem like a good way to force yourself to save money. But who wants a savings account that earns zero interest and that you can't get to in an emergency? If you get a large refund every year, go to your personnel office and change your withholding.

Then set up a savings account and have the extra money deposited directly into the savings account. By the end of the year, you will have the amount of your tax refund—plus interest.

Seek professional help. If you itemize deductions, are self-employed, sold a house, or have any other special schedules to fill out, you may benefit by hiring a certified public accountant (CPA) or tax preparer to complete your tax return. The preparer could save you more money in taxes than the fee charged. A good professional tax preparer spends hundreds of hours working on tax returns and attending seminars and continuing education courses. If you do hire someone to fill out your return, be sure that the preparer has other clients in situations similar to yours. That will tell you that he or she has the background to know how to find all the deductions you are allowed.

> Nothing is certain but death and taxes.
>
> Benjamin Franklin
> (1706-1790)

Keep organized records. Whether you complete your tax return yourself or hire someone, you will be ahead of the game if you keep neat, organized records all year long. If you do prepare your own taxes, you will save yourself time and headaches. If you hire a tax preparer, be sure to schedule an appointment early in the year. Your preparer will be able to set up a bookkeeping system for you in a manner that will save time and money. Expect to pay more to have your tax return completed if you dump off a grocery bag full of receipts that are not organized at all. You may overlook a large deduction if your receipts are unorganized.

Negotiate the fee. Be sure to ask the tax preparer about ways to keep the fee as low as possible, and negotiate the fee up front. You probably will not be able to negotiate the fee with a large firm or a tax preparation chain, but a local CPA firm or bookkeeping service might be willing to negotiate a lower rate.

Try tax preparation software. If you have a computer, one of the tax software programs might make the job easier and would be cheaper than going to a CPA. Most tax programs cost less than $50 and should handle most people's tax situations.

Seek knowledge. No one knows your special tax circumstances better than you do. Don't rely on your tax preparer to be a mind reader. You must become aware of the kind of information you need to pass on. Ask questions and be sure to mention any financial changes that have occurred over the year. Things that seem insignificant might have a big impact on the taxes you may owe.

Don't rely on the IRS toll-free number for information. Many times the information they give you will NOT be accurate. If you do follow their advice, be sure to write down when you called, whom you talked to, and exactly what the person said. If you can prove you got wrong information from the IRS, you won't pay a penalty, but you will still be liable for any additional taxes owed.

Consider filing separate returns. If you are married, don't automatically assume that as a couple you will pay the least tax with a joint return. If you are a two-income family and one of you has high medical expenses, you may be able to save a substantial amount of tax by filing separately. Always calculate it both ways and see which results in the least amount of taxes for both of you.

Shift income. If you receive investment income or you have a capital gain to declare, you may want to check out the rules on shifting or transferring some of the income or gain to your children. You may be able to save some taxes by having it taxed at their rate— probably 15 percent—instead of your higher rate.

Remember, honesty is the best policy. Always take all the deductions you are legally allowed. Taking deductions that you are not entitled to can be very dangerous to your pocketbook. If you get audited down the road, you will owe the additional tax, penalties, and tons of interest. The audit could occur when you can least afford it. Cheating the government out of its taxes can be a very expensive mistake.

> A budget is a financial schedule adopted to prevent part of the month being left at the end of your money.
>
> Anonymous

Don't wait until April 14. Fill out your tax return as soon as you have all the needed information. If you owe money, you can plan for the expense rather than getting a nasty surprise at the last minute. If you are owed a refund, you can file early and get your refund early. If you owe, wait until early April to file and earn interest on your money in the meantime.

Review your return. Always check the return for accuracy before you mail it off to the IRS. Recheck the math. Make sure all your dependents' social security numbers are listed. If you file a joint return, be sure that both of you sign the return.

Send your return via certified mail. Certified mail costs money, but anything can happen. Keep the receipt with your copy of your return. If the government claims that you were late with your return and wants to charge you interest, you have proof you sent it in on time.

If you have your taxes done by a tax preparation service, think twice before you opt for the "instant refund" loan the service provides. When you put the numbers to these loans, the annual interest can translate into a whopping 50 to 100 percent!

Respond immediately if you receive a notice from the IRS. Interest and penalties will be added to your account from day one. If you wait long enough, your wages will be garnisheed or your bank accounts will be frozen. Call the number listed on the notice and find out what the problem is. If you did make an error on your tax return and you do not have enough money to pay the entire amount due, work out a payment plan. Remember, the longer you draw out the payments the more interest you will have to pay, so it is to your advantage to pay off the taxes as soon as possible.

SUMMER

Summer is a busy time of the year. The kids are out of school and will want to be entertained. You'll need to pull some low-cost entertainment tricks out of your hat. Most of us will head out for a vacation during the summer months. A vacation can be both fun and frugal if you know some tips that will make your vacation easier to pay for. Outside activities are also typical summer fare. Save money on barbecuing in your backyard, keeping your lawn looking great, and keeping the pests away from your picnics. The biggest summer expense of all is air conditioning—get some hints on keeping cool on the cheap and many other ways to save during the summer.

KEEP YOUR COOL

Air conditioning your house can raise your electric bills to astronomical levels. But there are ways you can keep your house cool and not pay the electric company a fortune. Use these tips to reduce the high cost of keeping cool.

Plant trees or shrubs to shade air conditioning units. The shade will help your air conditioning unit perform more efficiently. After planting the trees or shrubs, keep them trimmed away from the unit so leaves or small branches won't get caught in the fan. Landscape your yard with trees that shade your house during the summer but let the sun through in the winter. Shade from trees is about seven times more effective than curtains at reducing air conditioning energy costs.

When you use air conditioning, set your thermostat as high as possible. An often recommended indoor temperature is 78 degrees Fahrenheit, which is reasonably comfortable and energy efficient. At 75 degrees you spend approximately 20 percent more on electricity, and at 72 degrees you spend approximately 40 percent more, than you would at a setting of 78 degrees.

Clean or replace air conditioning filters once a month during the hot summer months. If the filter is dirty, the fan has to run longer to remove the same amount of air, which uses up more electricity.

To save money, set the air conditioning fan speed on high except in very humid weather. When it's humid, set the fan speed at low; you'll get less cooling, but more moisture will be removed from the air—which will make it feel cooler.

Don't place lamps or a television set near the air conditioner's thermostat. Heat from these appliances can trick your air conditioning unit into running longer than necessary.

Don't air condition your fireplace opening. In summer, as in winter, fireplace openings can be a source of lost energy dollars. Close the damper and check and promptly repair any leaks.

Do all you can to keep the bright daytime sun out. Close the draperies, blinds, or shades on all windows during the heat of the day. Outside vertical louvers, awnings, or shutters offer even greater blocking power. If you live in a warm, sunny climate, louvers, awnings, or shutters will quickly pay for themselves in saved electricity.

If possible, use your stove, clothes dryer, and other heat-generating appliances in the early morning or late evening hours, when it's cooler outside. On hot days serve uncooked dishes. What's more, the cold food will probably be more appealing in the heat. If you have them, use energy-saving appliances such as electric cooking pots, microwaves, and pressure cookers instead of heating up the house with the oven or stove. You'll stay cooler and dramatically cut your energy costs.

Savings out the Window

Turn off window air conditioners when you leave a room for more than two hours. It takes less energy to cool the room down later than to leave the unit running. An inexpensive timer can be used to turn the unit back on half an hour before you get home.

An electric fan used with your window air conditioning unit can spread the cooled air farther without greatly increasing your power use. But be sure the air conditioner is powerful enough to help cool the additional space.

The Frugal Fan

An attic fan can drastically reduce your need for air conditioning. As warm air rises to the attic, the fan blows it out of the house. Studies show that an attic fan can shorten the amount of time you use air conditioning by 30 to 50 percent without sacrificing comfort. In the warmer southern climates, this can translate into a savings of $100 to $200 each year. In the cooler northern climates, you may not even have to turn the air conditioning on! At low to moderate humidity levels, an attic fan can make your house comfortable when it's up to 85 degrees outside.

When turning on the air conditioning, don't set your thermostat at a colder setting than normal. The house will not cool down any faster; it will merely cool to a lower temperature, thus using more energy.

Every hour you have an attic fan on and the air conditioning off, you save money. If you're paying 8 cents a kilowatt-hour for electricity, you can run a 400-watt attic fan for about 3 cents per hour. Compare that to the 34 cents it costs to run a typical three-ton-capacity air conditioner for an hour. An attic fan can be installed for $250 to $600, depending on its size and quality. If you live in a warm climate, you could save enough money on your electric bills to pay for the unit in less than two years.

Savings on the Ceiling

One of the main ways our bodies stay cool is through evaporation. Anything we can do to speed up evaporation will make us feel cooler.

KEEP YOUR COOL

If you don't have an attic fan, you can get a similar cooling effect on a smaller scale from a ceiling fan. By moving air around the room, the ceiling fan speeds evaporation and makes you feel cooler. That allows you to keep the thermostat set a little higher, resulting in a lower cooling bill. Here's how you can get the most savings from your ceiling fan:

- When buying a fan, look for one with a variable speed control that allows you to adjust the blade speed to provide the amount of cooling you desire.
- Ceiling fans are most effective when mounted seven to eight feet above the floor. In a high-ceilinged room, use an extension rod from the ceiling to hang the fan at the proper height.
- In the summertime, set the switch so that the fan rotates clockwise. This brings the warm air up toward the ceiling.
- A ceiling fan doesn't cool the air or the furniture in a room. It cools only you. So use a ceiling fan only when you are in the room. Turn it off when you leave, just as you would a light.

More Summer Energy Savers

Turn off your water heater when you go out of town. Any time you will be away for more than two days, this will save you money. In the summer, reheating the water is much cheaper than keeping it hot.

Keep your freezer full. A half-empty freezer uses much more energy to keep cold. During the summer it's easy to keep a freezer full. To fill up the space, store ice cubes and make large blocks of ice in clean plastic milk cartons. The ice will come in handy for use in coolers and for backyard barbecues.

SUMMER BEST BUYS CALENDAR

June

Apricots, asparagus, beans, beef, beets, berries, cherries, corn, cucumbers, eggs, fish, lemons, melons, peas, plums, radishes, salmon, summer squash, tomatoes, women's sportswear, furniture, luggage, lingerie, summer sportswear, building materials.

July

Apricots, beans, beets, berries, cherries, corn, cucumbers, grapes, fish, lemons, limes, melons, nectarines, plums, peppers, squash, tomatoes, watermelon, underwear, shoes, formal wear, men's summer suits, bathing suits, jewelry, air conditioners, fuel oil, home appliances.

August

Beans, chicken, corn, eggplant, fish, grapes, melons, lemons, peaches, pears, plums, peppers, summer squash, tomatoes, watermelon, furniture, carpet, linens, air conditioners, gardening tools, sporting goods, patio furniture, new cars, camping equipment, home furnishings.

BE A BUDGET BRIDE

A wedding can be a wonderful, memorable, once-in-a-lifetime event, but it can also be financially devastating. A young couple should think ahead to what is really important to them and spend their money accordingly. Of course most brides would like to have a beautiful wedding with memories that will last a lifetime, but it's not necessary to spend a fortune for it. You can have a lovely wedding inexpensively.

Your Dress

There are many different ways to cut expenses on a wedding dress. You can ask to borrow a dress from a friend or relative. A vintage wedding gown from your mother or an aunt can be beautiful, fashionable, and very frugal. Another money-saving option is to rent a dress from a local formal shop. Look in the telephone book under formal wear. They typically have very expensive gowns that you can rent for a small fraction of the price you would pay to purchase the gown. Bridal shops often have discontinued dresses for sale at greatly reduced prices. You can also shop at thrift or consignment shops. If you find a secondhand dress you like that is not your exact size, chances are it can easily be altered to fit. It is very easy to alter a dress that is slightly loose to fit perfectly.

Flowers

Flowers can add up to big dollars. Why not make your own flower arrangements out of silk flowers? Shop flea markets and discount stores for inexpensive silk flowers.

Instead of buying a large bouquet of flowers, carry a single long-stemmed rose, or several of them. Some baby's breath around the roses will add some flair without adding much cost.

Bridesmaids

The bridesmaids do not have to wear the same dress or even the same color dress. Why not have a "rainbow" wedding and let the bridesmaids pick out their own dress—or wear one they already have in their closet? Depending on the style of dresses, a lace collar or some trim may be added to make the dresses look similar to each other.

Ushers

Instead of renting tuxedos, why not have the men wear dark-colored suits? Matching ties and a simple carnation as a boutonniere will make the suits look more formal.

Photographs

Ask a friend or relative to take the wedding pictures. If you do not know any real camera buffs, ask two people to take pictures at your wedding. Between the two, they are bound to get some good pictures. Many times the person asked to do this will give the pictures to the bride and groom as their wedding gift. Offer to buy the film and pay for the developing.

Having a professional videographer is common at weddings these days. The price for this service ranges from $500 to $2,000. Find a friend with a video camera to record the ceremony and part of the reception. Offer to pay for the videotapes.

The reception

For the reception, have a picnic, potluck, or barbecue, or just serve hors d'oeuvres instead of serving a formal meal. Everyone will enjoy the relaxed atmosphere, and you'll save a ton of money.

Buy the wedding cake from a local vocational school. It will be very inexpensive—usually slightly more than the cost of the supplies. If you can't find a vocational school in your area that makes wedding cakes, check with local grocery stores or a bakery instead of a caterer. Call around for the best price. Buy a small tiered wedding cake and make some extra sheet cakes to serve to the guests.

> That man is richest whose pleasures are the cheapest.
>
> Anonymous

You can find many decorating items such as the bride and groom for the cake and paper wedding bells at discount party stores.

If you buy printed invitations, choose regular to small-sized ones. They'll cost less, and you'll avoid paying the extra postage that the large-sized ones require. Don't order thank-you notes with your invitations. Buy low-cost thank-you notes or plain cards from a discount store for a fraction of the cost.

Be sure to allow yourself enough time. You must start planning early. If you don't have enough time to shop around for the best prices, you may end up paying more than you really want to.

THRIFTY TRAVEL TIPS

Money spent on an annual vacation is well worth it; the trick is to make sure you get value for your dollars. With good planning, you can enjoy a summer vacation without overspending.

Planning the Getaway

Use a travel agent to help you plan your trip. A good travel agent can save you money by searching for bargain destinations and looking out for good deals. A travel agent should be able to make travel suggestions that will get you the most for your travel dollars. Let them know you are looking for a bargain and see what they suggest. You may be pleasantly surprised.

After you have decided on a destination, call the local Chamber of Commerce or tourism bureau and ask for tourist information, brochures, maps, and any other information about the area. Most tourism bureaus have a toll-free number. Call toll-free information (1-800-555-1212) to see if a toll-free number is available. This information will make planning your trip easier and will tell you what free and low-cost activities the area has to offer. You'll probably get discounts offered by local attractions, restaurants, and other local businesses.

Pick a destination that has lots of free activities (such as parks, museums, or historical sites). You can have fun, learn something interesting, and save money.

Many families travel in summer because that's when the children are out of school, but for that reason it is the most expensive time to travel. If you can travel during the off-season, you'll avoid crowds and save the most money. October to April is the off-season for most areas. Lodging and all attractions should be discounted 30 to 50 percent off during the off-season. Call ahead to find out when the off-season rates for your destination begin and how much you will save.

Check your car before heading out on a trip. If needed, tune it up and change the oil. Make sure your spare tire is filled with air. Check fluids, air pressure in tires, belts, and any other problem areas. This will help avoid an expensive out-of-town breakdown.

> The best place to spend your vacation is just inside your income.
>
> Anonymous

Check with the American Association of Retired Persons, if you are a member, or your auto club for travel advice, discounts, maps, and other services. Both have lots of ways to help you save money.

If you're traveling by car on the interstates, post a list on the dashboard of the major cities you will travel through. After a stop, you can glance at it quickly when you get back on the highway to make sure you are headed in the right direction. One wrong turn can lead you miles out of the way, wasting time and gas.

The Lowdown on Lodging

Book reservations at least three weeks in advance; rates are often 40 to 50 percent lower.

Book reservations directly with the hotel. Central reservation services that answer calls for all the hotels in a chain may not know about special deals available at the particular hotel you will be staying at.

If you will be staying for a full week at your destination, try to find a condo or vacation cottage to rent instead of a hotel room. The rate will probably be cheaper, and you'll have much more space and the extra added benefit of a full kitchen.

Always bargain for hotel rates. Ask about several rates such as senior citizen discounts, a corporate rate, a weekend rate, or a group discount offered to members of clubs or associations. Ask if they have any special promotional rates. When they find out that you are insistent about saving money, they will work harder to find you the lowest rate.

Always review your lodging, car rental, or any other travel bills closely. Frequently you can find errors. Ask for clarification of any charges you are not certain about.

Take a Bite Out of Your Travel Budget

Eat a big breakfast when traveling and go lighter on lunch and dinner. Breakfast is typically the least expensive meal of the day.

If you're traveling by car, always take a cooler along filled with drinks, snacks, and even quick meals such as sandwiches to keep your food costs under control. Find a nice roadside picnic area and enjoy a family picnic instead of spending big money each day on restaurant meals. You can shop along the way to replenish supplies.

Don't eat at the hotel restaurant where you are staying. You can usually get a better meal at a nearby restaurant for much less.

For a quick travel lunch, arrange a sandwich, carrot sticks, fruit, and a cookie or other snack on a clean Styrofoam tray. Cover the tray with plastic wrap. Make one for each person traveling. The tray makes it easy to eat anywhere, even if you can't find a roadside table.

Order ice water to drink with restaurant meals. It should be free, and not ordering soft drinks will really make a difference in the total tab.

Take your own coffeepot and supplies to make fresh coffee in the hotel or motel each morning. You can even go a step further and take items such as a toaster and an electric skillet. Some families really economize on meals and spend the bulk of the vacation budget on special attractions—or take a longer vacation.

Stop at the state welcome center and pick up a discount hotel booklet. Many states offer a discount booklet for rooms that would otherwise go empty. The rates in these booklets are really a bargain.

Deals for Your Travel Wheels

When renting a car, reserve the lowest rate you can find on a compact car. You can almost always upgrade the car when you arrive, and often the upgrade will be free. Most car rental companies have many more mid-sized and large cars than small ones. If a compact car is not available when you check in, ask for a free upgrade to a larger car.

Call your insurance company before renting a car to find out if you are insured while driving a rental. The insurance that rental agencies sell is expensive and is not necessary if you are already covered.

When you turn the car in, don't opt for the rental car company to refill the gas tank. It may sound like a bargain, but in reality they will charge you for a full tank of gas even if the car has some gas in it. Fill the gas tank up yourself before returning the rental car to make sure you don't overpay.

Do Sweat the Small Stuff

Here are some little ways to save while traveling.

Take along postcard stamps. They are cheaper than stamps for first class letters. Trying to find postcard stamps on vacation wastes valuable time.

Always buy more film than you think you'll need when it is on sale at home. You can spend double or even triple the amount if you wait and buy while on vacation.

HOW TO FLY FOR LESS

1. Look for airfare bargains right after Christmas, Thanksgiving, or Easter.

2. Summertime is also a great time to search for airfare bargains, because business travel falls off. Scan your local newspaper for special deals such as buy-one-get-one-free offers.

3. Plan ahead. To get most of the bargain fares you need to buy tickets 21 days in advance.

4. Be flexible with your schedule. Staying over a Saturday can drastically reduce your fare. When making reservations, tell the operator that you are looking for a bargain fare. Ask what you have to do to get their lowest rate.

5. Make friends with a travel agent. They can let you know in advance when bargain fares are going to be offered.

6. If you are flying to attend a funeral or family medical emergency, ask the airline about special fares under their bereavement policy. They will need some proof, such as a funeral notice or a letter from the doctor, but if you qualify it could save you a bundle.

THRIFTY TRAVEL TIPS

Use a pay phone to make calls rather than pay the hotel fee to use your room phone. Some hotels have extremely high phone rates for long-distance charges. You never know what the rate is going to be. Use a calling card with your regular long-distance company to save the most.

Use rest areas for breaks. They have free water and clean rest rooms—and no restaurants or gift shops to tempt you to spend more money.

Before you leave on your trip, buy books and magazines to read on vacation at used book stores or garage sales. A new book bought at the airport will cost at least $5 for a paperback. Be prepared with your own magazines and books to read during any layovers or delays.

Consolidate and Save

An easy way to save money on travel is to use a consolidator. If they have what you're looking for, the price should make you happy. Consolidators buy airline tickets, hotel rooms, or tours that are projected to not sell at the full retail price. The company selling the tickets, tours, or rooms figures that selling to a consolidator at a deep discount is better than leaving the room or seat empty.

Airline consolidators buy seats on regularly scheduled flights at rock-bottom prices. Then they add a markup and sell the tickets to the general public at a savings of 20 to 50 percent off the regular fares. Many consolidators advertise in newspaper travel sections. Or try calling UniTravel, a well-established consolidator, at 1-800-325-2222. Always pay with a credit card so you'll have a record of the transaction.

Hotel consolidators can cut the cost of a room by as much as 40 percent. After you've called and negotiated your best price, call the hotel consolidators and see if you can get a lower rate. Call Hotel Reservations Network at 1-800-964-6835 or Quikbook at 1-800-789-9887. Both list lodgings in more than 20 large American cities that are frequent travel destinations.

Frugal Photo Finishing

For developing the film from your summer vacation or any other film you can use a mail-order processor and wait a week or two. Or you can drop your film off at a supermarket, drugstore, or camera store for pickup in a couple of days. A third option is take your film to a minilab. A minilab is a retail outlet that does the film processing on the premises and usually offers finished prints in about an hour. While the minilabs are fast, they are almost always more expensive than dropping your film off for processing by a big laboratory or mail-order processing.

PICTURE PERFECT				
Exposures	Super-market	Drug store	Discount store	One-hour developer
12	$2.79	$5.89	$2.62	$6.00
24	5.99	10.19	4.94	9.60
36	8.09	14.89	6.88	13.20

Prices for double prints or larger 4×6 photos were compared, since some supermarkets offer only these premium services. The best price for single prints, offered by a discount drug store, was $1.33 for 12 exposures, $2.72 for 24 exposures, and $3.67 for 36 exposures.

The main drawback to mail-order film processing is the time it takes to get your prints back. And solving problems that require reprinting can be awkard and very time consuming from a distance. You are also required to prepay the cost of developing. If all your prints do not come out, you will get a coupon to use on your next purchase instead of getting a cash refund. Prices for mail-order film processing are comparable to the lowest prices you can find locally.

Know Where to Go

Prices on film developing can vary dramatically. One supermarket might charge double what another store charges. Some force you to buy two prints or larger prints to get the price higher. Before you drop film off, always compare prices. Why pay double for the same service?

Shop the Sales

If you are not in a big hurry to get your film processed, wait for an advertised sale. Many grocery stores and discount stores will advertise 50 percent off film developing the week after a holiday. They may also run the sale once or twice during the summer to encourage shoppers to bring in vacation photo finishing. The store hopes of course that you will shop in the store when you drop the photos off and again when you pick them up.

Refund a Bundle

Have your film processed at a store that will give you a refund for any pictures that do not come out or that you are not happy with. Most grocery stores and discount stores will refund your money, but they may not advertise the fact. All you have to do is ask. This is especially important if you are just learning how to use your camera or you are teaching a child how to take pictures.

A Photo Opportunity

No matter where you have your film processed, machines do most if not all of the labor. It's important to review your prints for processing defects. Although someone at the processor should be quality-checking your photos, many labs skip that step or do it only cursorily, depending on the workload.

If you find a print that is unsatisfactory, check the negative. You can't expect a processor to be able to do much with a badly exposed negative. But if the image on the negative has good contrast, ask to have the print remade. Give them clear instructions—tell them the car is fire-engine red, not pink, for example. You should not be charged for these reprints.

Unfortunately there is no remedy for film that's ruined by the processor. You can expect to get a new roll of film and free processing for that roll. If your film is lost, chances are good that it will eventually turn up. You can increase the chances of it being found by writing your name and address on the film cartridge before turning it in for processing.

TINY TIGHTWADS

Financial experts predict that to raise a child to 18 years of age will cost well over $200,000, and if you have college aspirations for your little ones, you'll need even more money. Of course they're worth it, but since kids are costly, it's important to save on their expenses and teach kids to be thrifty too.

Clothes on the Cheap

Remember that until about the age of eight, kids couldn't care less where you buy their clothing. As they get older, they will become more picky about it. Take advantage of your children's younger years to save money shopping at thrift stores, getting hand-me-downs from friends and relatives, and buying from discount stores.

Buy clothes for children in durable fabrics that will stand up to a lot of wear. Avoid thin, flimsy fabrics and poorly applied trimmings. Novelty items glued onto shirts will probably come off in the washing machine.

Choose clothes with an elastic waist or without a defined waistline—the clothes will grow with the child.

If you have, or plan to have, more than one child, buy durable clothes that can be passed down to either sex. You can make clothes handed down from a brother more feminine for a girl by adding some lace around the collar or sleeves.

Recycle worn winter pajamas into summer sleepwear by cutting off legs to make shorts and cutting long sleeves into shorter sleeves. Or cut them completely off for sleeveless sleepwear.

Store kids' outgrown clothes in labeled boxes to keep them organized. They can easily be found and passed down to younger siblings.

Putting some effort into extending the life of kids' clothes can save quite a bit of money. Constantly replacing outfits that have been ruined by stains or tears will really add up.

Inspect clothing often for small tears or seams that are starting to unravel. Take care of small problems quickly so they don't get worse.

Try to buy play clothes in darker colors or prints that will not show stains as easily. Make sure your kids change into their play clothes when they come home from school.

Make sure that each child has at least one outfit to be worn only for church or other special occasions. You'll avoid paying full price for a special-occasion outfit purchased at the last minute.

Frugal Food for the Wee Ones

Compare the price of a school lunch to that of packing your own. Depending on what you pack and the price in your school district, you may save money buying a school lunch instead of packing one.

Wash and refill glass or plastic bottles with inexpensive lemonade or juice made from concentrate. The glass or plastic bottles usually hold more than the little boxes of juice, and even your teenagers will like drinking from them.

Kids love ice cream treats. Instead of buying expensive novelty ice cream treats at the grocery store or from the ice cream truck, make your own. Buy a low-cost gallon of ice cream and some cones. Dip the ice cream into the cones and let them freeze hard. Lay the cones on a sheet of waxed paper until they are hard, and then wrap in a plastic bag. For an extra-special treat, you can dip them in chocolate or sprinkles. By making a bunch of them at one time, you have ready-made treats whenever the kids ask for them. When the ice cream truck drives by and the kids start begging for a treat, simply pull one of your cones out of the freezer.

Make your own low-cost fudge bars. Freeze chocolate milk in ice-pop containers and save a bundle. You can buy the plastic ice-pop containers at grocery and discount stores.

Don't spend big bucks on frozen microwave breakfasts for kids. When you make pancakes, waffles, or French toast, make an extra batch and freeze them. Your homemade breakfast entrees will heat up just as quickly, and they probably will have more flavor.

Frugal Fun

Bath-time sponges for kids in animal shapes and other shapes are at least twice the price of regular sponges. Buy inexpensive foam sponges and cut your own shapes. For more low-cost bath-time fun, add a drop or two of food coloring to the water. You can turn the tub into a blue ocean, a green lake, or a pink paradise.

Save plastic strawberry baskets and use them to entertain youngsters. Dip them in soapy water and then wave them through the air. A cloud of bubbles will appear. This will entertain children for hours, and the cost is minimal.

When you take your children to the library, take all the date-due cards out of the books and put them in a plastic bag. Hang the plastic bag near your calendar. Make a note on the calendar when the books are due so you can make sure they are returned without a fine. When you have matched up each card with a book, you know you have rounded up all the books that were checked out.

Stringing macaroni is fun and much cheaper than buying bead kits. To make colored macaroni, combine 2 tablespoons rubbing alcohol, a few drops of food coloring, and a handful of pasta in a plastic zip-lock bag. Work the pasta around in the bag until it is dyed. Dump the contents onto newspaper and allow to dry. To make stringing easier, wrap one end of the string with a piece of clear plastic tape to keep it stiff.

Toys for Tots

A good source for low-cost toys is hand-me-downs from friends and relatives. When you mention you are looking for toys, you'll probably get more freebies than junior has time to play with.

Buy preowned toys from secondhand stores, thrift shops, garage sales, or flea markets. Many times you can find used toys that look just like new. Some need just a little cleaning to look nearly new.

Buy toys that are well constructed and made to last. Some toys are prone to damage by little ones as soon as they come out of the package, and other toys can last long enough to be passed down to the next generation. Avoid fragile items that are bound to get broken before Santa gets back to the North Pole.

Finger Paints

    2 cups cold water
    ¼ cup cornstarch
    Food coloring
    Liquid dishwashing detergent

Mix cold water and cornstarch in a small saucepan; boil until thick. Let cool slightly before pouring into small containers (baby-food jars work great). Add a couple of drops of food coloring to each container. Add a drop of liquid dishwashing detergent to each container to make clean-up easy. Let the paints cool to room temperature before using.

Thrifty Play-dough Recipe

1 cup flour
½ cup salt
2 tablespoons cream of tartar
1 cup water
1 tablespoon vegetable oil

Mix flour, salt, and cream of tartar in a medium saucepan. Add water and oil. Cook over medium heat for 3 to 5 minutes or until it becomes the consistency of dough. Let cool and add a few drops of food coloring if desired. Store in an airtight container or plastic bag. The kids will have many hours of inexpensive fun playing with the dough. This is always a great rainy-day project.

Ice Packs

Summertime usually means more bumps and bruises. Make your own ice packs and keep them ready in the freezer to soothe the aches and pains. To make a small ice pack, use a quart-size plastic zip-lock bag. Pour one cup rubbing alcohol and two cups water into the bag and squeeze out as much air as possible before you press the bag closed. Place the bag in the freezing compartment and leave it there until you need it. The alcohol-and-water mixture will not freeze solid; it stays slushy and can be shaped around difficult places such as knees or elbows. You can reuse these

SCHOOL SUPPLIES

Kids can be entertained for hours without expensive toys. These low-cost activities will encourage creativity.

- A large cardboard box such as a large appliance box makes a terrific playhouse or fort. It can entertain kids for days—even weeks.

- Collect colorful junk mail for children to play with. They'll spend hours cutting out pictures and pasting them on paper. The stickers from magazine solicitations are especially fun to punch out and stick on paper.

- Used computer paper or other office paper that is printed on only one side is perfect for drawing and coloring. Bring a big stack home and let your little artists get to work.

- Have the kids play cash register or bank teller by making play money out of the cardboard that comes in pantyhose and shirts. Trace coins on the cardboard and draw coin designs. Cut out the coins and color them. Save a clean, empty egg carton and fill it with the play money.

- Give children old magazines and newspapers and ask them to cut out all the coupons inside. Then you can quickly go through the pile and decide which ones you want to keep. Show them how much you save with some of the coupons, and you'll have an eager coupon-clipper helper.

- Keep a box of old clothes that children can use to play dress-up. You can use old items from your closet. A few dresses, old white men's shirts, high-heeled shoes, cheap jewelry, ties, purses, and other miscellaneous items create a boxful of entertainment.

bags many times. To make a large ice pack, use a gallon-size bag and double the recipe.

Q. My three-year-old has left several items of crayon "art" around the house that I would like to remove. Some of the drawings are on painted walls, and a few are on wallpaper. How can I remove crayon marks from the walls?

A. On painted walls, especially white walls, regular white toothpaste usually works well. Rub a dab of toothpaste on the crayon marks and wash away with warm water. For large drawings and wallpaper, you may want to try removing the crayons with a hair dryer. Use a hair dryer set on low to warm the marks for a few seconds, then wipe the area clean with a damp cloth.

Budget Baby

It seems that the smaller they are the more they cost. The cost of feeding, clothing, and diapering a little one can be astounding. Here are some ways to save.

Make your own baby food. Puree home-cooked foods in a food processor or blender, and freeze individual portions in an ice cube tray. Transfer the baby-food cubes into freezer bags.

Breast feeding is considered to be the best method of feeding a baby, and of course it is the thriftiest way to go. However, millions of infants thrive on the bottle—especially if Mommy has to return to work quickly. If you choose to bottle feed, remember that powdered formulas are much cheaper than ready-mixed formulas.

Don't spend money on shoes for infants. Most pediatricians agree that babies really need bare feet to get a good balance on the floor while they are learning to walk. Once they have mastered the art of walking, it's time to buy a pair of shoes.

Compare the cost of cloth diapers versus disposable diapers. Parents know that disposable diapers are a big expense, but many parents enjoy the convenience they offer. You also have the option of using a diaper service that will wash and deliver clean diapers to your home for a monthly fee. While the service costs substantially more than washing cloth diapers yourself, it is usually cheaper than buying disposable diapers. Plus, of course, it eliminates the waste of throwing all those disposable diapers away. Consider your options.

Make your own baby wipes. Here's how:

Homemade Baby Wipes

1 to 1½ cups water
1 tablespoon baby shampoo
1 tablespoon baby oil or canola oil
1 roll of paper towels cut in half to produce 2 small rolls

In a plastic container with a lid, combine water, baby shampoo, and oil. Place one of the small paper towel rolls in the container to soak up the liquid. When towels are soaked through, remove the cardboard tube and pull wipes from the center. You may need to add more liquid if the paper towels are not soaked all the way through. Save the other small roll of paper towels for next time.

Thrifty Kids

Teaching children to handle money and make smart money choices will benefit both the child and the adult. It is never too soon to start teaching your children the value of a dollar.

Give your children a list of chores to complete before you give them their allowance. This will help them learn the concept of earning money. If they don't finish the list or don't do the chores properly, deduct from their allowance. You can bet that next time they'll get it done on time and the correct way.

Take your kids to garage sales and teach them how to bargain for what they want to buy. Kids can be taught how to be smart shoppers very early. This is a skill that they can use for the rest of their lives.

Put your children in charge of saving aluminum cans and glass bottles for deposits. Let them make the returns and keep the money.

ROLL AWAY SAVINGS

Little children and playful cats or dogs love to watch a roll of toilet tissue spin off the roll. Foil them by squeezing the roll together, so it is no longer round, before inserting the new roll of tissue on the holder. This will also keep everyone in the house from pulling off and using more paper than is needed.

Encourage children to start a small business to make money. This will require some work from you, since you will have to be their "not so silent" business partner, but the rewards should be worth it. They will learn responsibility and work ethics and also earn some extra money. Kids can mow grass, baby-sit, walk and feed pets, clean houses, do ironing, trim trees and bushes, wash windows, wash cars, clean out attics and garages, and do just about any other project that adults would rather pay a youngster to do. To get the word out in the neighborhood that they are hardworking and willing to tackle almost any job, the kids can print up flyers and place them in neighbors' mail-boxes. You will need to supervise to make sure that your child is safe and is being paid a reasonable amount for the work performed. As children get older and wiser about working, you won't have to be as involved.

Once a child starts making money, encourage them to start a savings account. Teach kids about both short-term saving and long-term saving. Let them save up for a large toy or game purchase and insist that some amount go into a college fund or other saving account.

FOOD, FABULOUS FOOD!

Whether your garden provides a bumper crop or you buy a bushel from a local farmer's market, if you freeze fruits and vegetables when they are fresh and in good condition, they should last one year frozen. Always store them in freezer bags or plastic freezer containers for the best results. Here's how to prepare your frozen assets.

Berries, grapes, cherries, peeled and sliced nectarines, plums, or peaches: To freeze fruit, lay prepared fruit in a single layer on a cookie sheet and freeze until firm. Then transfer the fruit into plastic freezer containers. By doing this you'll be able to thaw out just the amount you need, since the fruit pieces will not be stuck together. Use without thawing in muffins, breads, cakes, and pies. Eat frozen cherries or grapes as a snack.

Tomatoes: Freeze whole, unpeeled, in a freezer container. Before using, drop in boiling water for a few seconds, then peel. Though they will be too mushy for salads, these tomatoes are perfect in cooked sauces, soups, and stews.

Green beans: Rinse; trim ends and cook in boiling water for 1 to 2 minutes. Pack into a freezer container. Use as a cooked vegetable or add to soups, stews, or casseroles.

Corn: Cook corn on the cob in boiling water for 3 minutes; cool and drain. Cut corn from cobs and freeze in a container. Serve as a cooked vegetable or stir into chowders, soups, fritters, or muffins.

Onions and peppers: Chop onions and peppers into small pieces and freeze on a cookie sheet (same method used for berries and other fruits). Transfer into a freezer container. Use frozen in recipes.

Frugal Fruit

Buy grapes when they are on sale and freeze them. Frozen grapes are a fun and nutritious snack that both children and adults will enjoy. Add frozen grapes to any type of punch to keep the drink cold without diluting it.

If you submerge a lemon, lime, or other citrus fruit in hot water for 15 minutes before squeezing, the fruit will yield almost twice as much juice. Or you can microwave the citrus fruit for 15 to 20 seconds before squeezing to get more juice.

When lemons or limes are bargain priced, buy extras and freeze the juice in ice cube trays. Remove the cubes and store in the freezer in a plastic bag. You can use the juice cubes when citrus fruit is out of season and the price is very high. You'll be surprised at how "fresh" the frozen juice tastes.

Instead of throwing citrus rinds away, freeze a few of the rinds whole. When a recipe calls for a zest of lemon or orange, you can use the frozen skin. Use a potato peeler to peel off small pieces of the rind. The frozen rind will be much easier to make into zest than a fresh one.

Vegetable Solutions

Don't throw away limp carrots or celery. To make them crisp again, soak the vegetables in ice-cold water for 30 minutes. The "re-crisped" vegetables will be crunchy and will taste just as good as fresh ones.

Instead of buying a steamer for vegetables, simply place the vegetables in a metal colander, place the colander over a saucepan of boiling water, and cover. It works just like a steamer but doesn't cost any more money or take up extra cabinet space.

When making mashed potatoes, save the water and add it back to the potatoes as you mash them. It is cheaper than adding milk, and your potatoes will be hot, creamy, and delicious.

Get more for your money when making mashed potatoes. Don't peel the potatoes. Just scrub and trim thoroughly, boil, and mash as usual. Unpeeled potatoes make healthful, delicious mashed potatoes.

Don't toss out leftover mashed potatoes. Freeze dollops of them and store in zip-lock freezer bags. You can use them later to make potato cakes or use them to thicken soups, stews, gravies, and sauces.

> The secret of thrift is to live as economically the day after payday as you do the day before.
>
> Anonymous

To speed baking time and save energy, cut baking potatoes in half and place them cut side down on a baking sheet before placing them in the oven. They will cook much faster this way. For added flavor, place a pat of butter or margarine under each half.

Store fresh mushrooms in a brown paper bag in the refrigerator. If you buy mushrooms in a plastic bag or package, take them out of the wrapping and place them into a paper bag to make them last longer. The paper bag absorbs some of the moisture and prevents spoilage. If you can't find a small paper bag, you can use paper towels.

To make onions last longer, don't store them near potatoes. Moisture from the potatoes will cause onions to sprout, and the onions will give your potatoes an off flavor. The best way to store onions is to hang them in old pantyhose. Drop the onions in the hose and tie a knot between each one. The onions will have enough air around them, and you can snip them off one at a time as you need them.

Get together with friends and neighbors and buy fruit and vegetables by the case from a wholesaler. They will be much fresher and lower in cost than what you can get at the grocery store.

Fried Green Tomatoes

At the end of the season, you'll find green tomatoes on your vine that will never ripen. Use them in this delicious recipe.

    1 cup flour
    1 teaspoon salt
    1 teaspoon pepper
    1 cup milk
    2 large or 3 small green tomatoes, sliced
  1⅓ cup vegetable oil

Combine flour, salt, and pepper in a small bowl. Place milk in a second bowl. Dip green tomato slices in milk, then dip them in flour mixture. Remove tomato slices to a plate and let them rest for 5 minutes. Dip them again in the flour mixture. Fry in vegetable oil over medium heat until brown, about 2 minutes on each side. Serve tomato slices hot.

Frozen Assets

When you buy frozen vegetables in a plastic bag, you should be able to feel the individual vegetables inside the bag. Don't buy a bag if you can't; the package probably has thawed at some point before being refrozen. The refrozen vegetables can have an off taste, their texture could suffer, and they will not have as many nutrients.

To make ice cream last longer, place a piece of waxed paper, plastic wrap, or aluminum foil on top of the ice cream once the container is opened. This will prevent ice crystals from forming on the ice cream and will keep it fresh-tasting longer.

To make inexpensive popping corn pop bigger and stay fresh longer, store it in the freezer. You don't even have to thaw out the popcorn before popping it.

Liquid Saving

To make low-cost frozen juice more appealing, mix it in the blender. This mixing method makes it a light and frothy drink. Pour the frothy drink into some special glasses and you have an inexpensive treat. Both children and adults will love it.

Instead of buying expensive flavored sparkling water, you can make your own. Buy store-brand or generic club soda and add a small amount of juice or a few drops of fruit extract (such as strawberry or lemon). This will make a low-calorie, inexpensive drink.

After opening a can of fruit, don't pour the juice down the drain. Instead, add the juice to your juice container in the refrigerator. You'll be adding more servings to your juice and adding flavor as well.

Freeze leftover tea, or any other drink your family likes, in ice cube trays. Use these cubes for a drink that does not get diluted as the ice melts.

If you prefer an expensive brand of coffee, try mixing your favorite brand half and half with a lower-priced brand. The rich flavors of your favorite brand will still come through. Maybe you won't be able to taste the difference.

After coffee has perked or dripped through, pour the hot coffee into a thermos bottle or a thermos coffee carafe that has been warmed with hot water. The coffee will stay hot without getting bitter, and you will save electricity.

Q. Is all bottled water spring water?

A. Many people pay extra for bottled water assuming it is spring water. If the label on bottled water does not specify that it comes from a natural spring, it is usually tap or well water that has been chemically treated and purified. You can buy purified drinking water from a machine for about 25 cents per gallon if you fill your own containers.

Marvelous Milk

You can extend the shelf life of milk about 10 days past the expiration date. If the milk is not spoiled before the expiration date, microwave, either in the carton or in a microwave container, on high until the temperature reaches 160 degrees. One cup of milk takes about 1½ minutes. Don't let the milk boil. Refrigerate immediately.

Another way to make milk last several days past the expiration date is to add a pinch of salt. The salt will not affect the taste of the milk, but it will keep it from spoiling as fast.

When milk starts to go sour, there's no need to throw it out. It's safe to use in cooking. Use it right away in cake batter, cookie dough, or pancake batter. You can also use it in recipes calling for buttermilk.

Instead of buying a carton of buttermilk for a recipe, add one tablespoon of vinegar to a cup of regular milk. Let the mixture stand for one half hour before using.

When you think the chocolate syrup container is completely empty, fill the container with milk and shake. You'll get every last bit of syrup out of the container. You can drink the chocolate milk cold or heat it for hot chocolate.

Cheese on the Cheap

Instead of throwing away hard cheese, grate it and use on your favorite vegetables and casseroles. Mix the hard cheese with stale bread crumbs for a delicious topping for vegetables and casseroles.

Cottage cheese will stay fresh longer if you store the carton upside down in the refrigerator. Just make sure the lid is on tight!

To prevent cheese from drying out, wrap it in a moist paper towel with a few drops of cider vinegar. Store the cheese in a sealed plastic bag or airtight container. You may need to add water or a drop or two of cider after a use or two.

Meat Marinade

Meat fibers are broken down and tenderized by vinegar. Less expensive cuts of meat can be used in most recipes without sacrificing flavor if they are tenderized. To tenderize meats, soak the meat in a cup of vinegar overnight; if desired, rinse off the vinegar before cooking.

Marinate meats in a plastic bag instead of a pan. By placing the meat in a bag, you will be able to use about half of the usual amount of marinade with the same results. Turn the bag over several times during the marinating process.

HOT OFF THE GRILL

Backyard barbecues are a summer staple. The food always seems to taste better when it's hot off the grill. You can spend a fortune buying charcoal briquettes, cleaning supplies for the grill, lava rocks, lighter fluids, and other supplies. Don't do it! There are ways to make your backyard barbecue a bargain.

If you use charcoal briquettes, don't let them continue to burn after you finish grilling. Remove the charcoal with tongs and place the briquettes into a large metal can with holes punched in it. Pour water over the coals and let them dry out. You can reuse the pieces of leftover charcoal for your next barbecue.

An easy and inexpensive way to clean a barbecue grill is to start while the grill is still warm. Dip newspapers in water and place the wet newspapers on top of the rack. Close the lid and let the newspapers stay on the rack for 20 to 45 minutes. When you open the lid, you will find that the newspapers have steam-cleaned your grill. Just rub the newspapers across the rack to make it clean and ready for the next barbecue. This method is quick, easy, and practically cost free. Tip: Don't let the newspapers stay on the grill for more than an hour; if allowed to dry on the grill, they will be hard to remove!

You don't have to replace the lava rocks in gas grills every year just because they get dirty and filled with grease. Instead of buying new ones, turn them upside down and turn the grill on high for about five minutes. Turning the rocks upside down allows the grease to drip out, which will clean the rocks and leave them as good as new!

An easy way to get charcoal briquettes started is to put several into a paper bag and light the bag. Or use a dry pine cone under the briquettes to get the fire started fast.

Instead of using lighter fluid, fill empty cardboard (not plastic) egg cartons with charcoal briquettes. Place them in the grill and light with a match; when they catch on fire, you will have a good arrangement of charcoal.

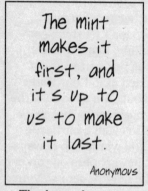

The mint makes it first, and it's up to us to make it last.

Anonymous

Use barbecue sauce only during the last 20 minutes of grilling. If you put it on too early, it will burn. To make your barbecue sauce go farther, add ⅓ cup water and ¼ cup sugar to one cup of barbecue sauce before brushing it on your meat. The result will be a sticky, yummy coating.

The best place to store your barbecuing utensils is in a bucket of sand. This will keep the tools from getting rusty and will make them last longer. Keep your small gardening tools rust-free by placing them in the bucket, too.

Save the ashes from charcoal grilling to add nutrients to your greenery. Sprinkle the completely cooled ashes over the dirt around your shrubs, grass, and plants, and watch your plants grow! It's like getting a free fertilizer.

Keep a water bottle close at hand to keep the fire under control. Don't waste your money on a special water bottle for the grill. You can use a clean liquid detergent bottle or any type of spray bottle.

MICROWAVE MAGIC

The popularity of microwave ovens is easily explained—they save both time and money. The cost of microwave ovens has also dropped dramatically to the point at which you can buy a very basic model for about $100. But you may be able to find a used microwave at a garage sale for a fraction of the cost. Many people tend to upgrade their microwaves before the oven wears out. One study by a power company found that for about 87 percent of your cooking tasks, doing them in a microwave oven can cut energy costs by at least 50 percent. During the hot summer you get the added bonus of not heating up the kitchen.

Fast and Frugal

Microwaves are most efficient at heating small to medium quantities of food. For example, to bake four potatoes, a microwave uses about 65 percent less energy than an electric oven. But on the other hand, to bring four cups of water to a boil, a microwave uses 10 percent more energy than an electric stove top.

It's true that you can spend lots of money on special cookware made especially for use in the microwave, but you can also be thrifty and find containers you already have on hand that work perfectly in the microwave. You can defrost foods right in their plastic freezer containers (with the lid off), as long as they are microwave-safe. You can heat bread or other items in straw serving baskets.

Most ceramic or glass casseroles and baking dishes for use in a regular oven also work just fine in the microwave oven. These types of cookware almost always cost less than dishes designed specifically for the microwave. Not only is it less expensive to use the same cookware in both the regular oven and the microwave, but you'll save on storage space as well.

To see if one of your nonmetal dishes or containers is usable in the microwave, put water in it and microwave on HIGH for about eight minutes. If the dish stays fairly cool to the touch, it's probably a good choice to use in the microwave. Don't use your best china or any dishes with metal trim in the microwave. Pottery may also be a poor choice to use in the microwave, since it can have metal in the glaze or impurities in the clay.

Not only are microwave ovens energy efficient, but they can cut down significantly on the amount of dirty dishes you have to wash. You can heat up a serving of hot chocolate right in the mug you'll drink it in. Cook vegetables right in their serving bowl. The microwave makes eating leftovers much easier and more appealing, since you can quickly put the leftovers on a plate and heat them up in just a minute or two. It makes leftovers a cheap fast food.

SOFTENING BROWN SUGAR

If your box of brown sugar is hard, don't throw it away. You can soften and freshen the brown sugar by placing the entire box in your microwave and heating it on HIGH (100%) power for about 20 seconds. Time will vary slightly depending on the amount of sugar in the box.

Bargain Bacon Cooker

Cook bacon the easy way without buying a special microwave bacon pan. Place a layer of clean paper towels on top of a brown grocery bag or several thicknesses of newspaper. Cook the bacon for 45 seconds to one minute per slice, or until done. The paper towels and the paper bag beneath will absorb most of the grease without wasting a bunch of paper towels. You'll end up with crisp bacon every time.

De-crystallizing Honey

You don't have to throw away honey that has formed crystals. Just place it in the microwave oven in a microwave-safe container. Insert a food probe, if your microwave has one, or a microwave-safe food thermometer. Microwave on HIGH (100%) power to 120°F. Watch the thermometer closely, because the honey will heat up quickly.

Drying Herbs

A number of herbs—dill, basil, parsley, sage, celery leaves, chives, mint, oregano, tarragon, or thyme—can quickly be dried in your microwave oven. The dried herbs taste better than store-bought dried herbs, and you'll pay a fraction of the cost. Here's what to do.

Take one small bunch of fresh herbs (about 4 or 5 stalks). Discard any discolored or decayed leaves. Rinse herbs in cold water; shake off excess. Pat dry completely.

Place a double layer of paper towels in the microwave. Do not use paper towels made from recycled paper, since the recycled material can contain small metal pieces. Spread herbs on paper towels. Place another paper towel over herbs. Microwave on HIGH (100%) power for 2 to 3 minutes. Check leaves for dryness by rubbing between paper towels to see if they crumble. If leaves are not dry, microwave for an additional 30 seconds at a time until dry. Remove from the microwave and allow to cool. Crumble herbs, discard any tough stems, and store in an airtight container.

Bargain Bread

To avoid making bread or rolls tough and dry, heat for about 15 seconds. Then heat for an additional few seconds if they are not hot. To prevent your muffins or pastries from getting soggy on the bottom, heat them on a paper towel.

Q. Can I pop regular popcorn in the microwave? The little microwave bags are so expensive.

A. Regular popcorn can be cooked in the microwave if you use a microwave-safe container made especially for popping corn. Don't try to pop it in a brown paper bag. Kernels can scorch and cause a fire inside the microwave oven if brown bags or other improper containers are used. Shop around; you should be able to find an inexpensive microwave popping container. It will quickly pay for itself if you enjoy popcorn.

ONE LAST BARGAIN

Death and funerals are not something we like to think about. But the truth is funerals are expensive, and you can wind up spending money needlessly when you are under the pressure of bereavement. A little planning ahead and forethought can save a significant amount of money.

Prepaid Savings

One way to save is to shop and pay for your own funeral expenses. This not only saves time and money; it assures your family members that you are being buried according to your wishes. All they have to do is make one phone call to the funeral home you have selected. Your family members will not have to agonize over the type of casket and service they think you would want. If you pick out an inexpensive service, your family knows that you wanted it that way. There is no second guessing.

Be aware that if the funeral home holding your pre-arrangement goes out of business, you are left with nothing. The safest way to pay for your funeral expenses in advance is to set up a trust fund through a bank for funeral expenses. Upon your death the bank will pay the proceeds of the trust to the funeral director with whom you have arranged your burial or cremation.

Tricks of the Trade

Believe it or not, funeral expenses are negotiable. The funeral home marks up expenses 250 to 500 percent. You need to think with your head and not let your grief get in the way when making funeral arrangements for a loved one. The difference you save will be felt in your wallet after the funeral. Openly tell the funeral director that you are going to check prices with other funeral homes in the area. This will let the funeral director know that you are willing to take your business somewhere else if you don't get a good price. Most funeral homes will refuse to be undersold by the competition around the block.

> *Taking it with you isn't nearly as important as making it last until you're ready to go.*
>
> Anonymous

However, before you do any price comparisons, it pays to ask who owns the funeral home. Today many large corporations have purchased hundreds of funeral homes as investments. Because the community has known the funeral home under its local name for so many years, the large corporation doesn't change its name. The "competition" around the corner may actually be owned by the same corporation.

You can expect to pay from $5,000 to $10,000 for a complete funeral. But how would you like to slash about $3,000 off your best negotiated price? If you are a United States veteran (or spouse or dependent of a veteran) with at least 90 days of service and an honorable discharge, you can be buried in a national cemetery, and the government will pay for the gravesite, the opening and closing of the grave, the vault, the marker, and perpetual care. These services are a benefit you get for serving your country.

Any funeral home director can make all the arrangements for a burial in a national cemetery. There are

114 different cemeteries across the nation. From the Arlington National Cemetery to your local national cemetery, they are among the most well-maintained, beautiful cemeteries in the nation. A veteran and spouse can be buried in the same gravesite, with one vault stacked on top of the other. Plus all minor children can be buried free. You would spend about $3,000 at a private cemetery for the services that the government will provide free for veterans and their dependents. Almost every family has veterans that could benefit from this "insider secret." You cannot, however, reserve space in advance at national cemeteries. Funeral directors making burial arrangements must apply for the space at the time of death.

Veterans and reservists are also eligible to receive a free American flag to drape over the casket. The flag will be given to the next of kin. Most funeral homes will tell you about the free flag, since it will not lower their profit. If you have a relative that is missing in action and presumed to be dead, the Veterans Administration will issue a flag on behalf of the service member. Flags are issued at VA regional offices, VA national cemeteries, and most local post offices.

For more information about burial benefits from the U.S. Government, contact the Department of Veterans Affairs at 810 Vermont Ave., N.W., Washington, DC 20420, and ask for the book *Federal Benefits for Veterans and Dependents.*

It's hard to be businesslike when you're grieving. Most people want to just make the preparations and worry about payment for services "later." You will thank yourself when "later" comes and you have been able to keep the funeral costs under control. These tips should open your eyes and help you or someone you love save money on funeral expenses.

FUN IN THE SUN

Your bathing suit will last longer if you always rinse it in cold water after swimming. This is especially important after swimming in a chlorinated pool. Chlorine can be very tough on clothing, making it fade and wear out very quickly.

Don't throw away old bed sheets; save them to take to the lake or the beach. They are much cooler to sit on than blankets, and it's easier to shake the sand and dirt off them.

Q. My hair is light, and sometimes during the summer it will turn slightly green when I swim in a pool. The special shampoos made for removing the green tint are very expensive. What inexpensive remedies can I use to remove the ugly green color?

A. The green tinge that light hair gets from the chlorine from a swimming pool is very easy to remedy. Just rub a little tomato juice on your hair, let it soak in for about two minutes, and wash as usual. You may be able to avoid the green tint altogether simply by taking a quick shower as soon as you are finished swimming.

The Sun Is Bright!

You may think a tan looks fashionable, but the unpleasant truth is that sunlight damages your skin even if you don't get sunburned. Ultraviolet radiation from the sun damages the elastin fibers in the skin, causing aging and a weather-beaten look. Sun damage is cumulative; signs of overexposure may not show up for 25 or 30 years. But the damage is irreversible.

Overexposure can also cause skin cancer, which is the most common form of cancer in the United States.

FUN IN THE SUN

One in seven Americans will develop skin cancer, and 90 percent of the cases are due to overexposure to the sun. Buying and using a sunscreen with a high sun-protection factor (SPF) is much cheaper in the long run that treating skin cancer. But if you do end up with a sunburn, try these low-cost remedies to make you feel better.

Instead of buying sunburn relief medicine, use plain old milk to get the best relief. Dip clean rags or wash-cloths in cold milk and place them over the sunburned areas. Leave the milk-soaked cloths in place for about 15 minutes. Milk really does soothe the pain. Use whole milk, because the fat content and the protein are what soothes irritated skin.

Advertisements may tell you that expensive sunglasses offer better eye protection than inexpensive ones, but the truth is they do not. Ophthalmologists generally agree that all you really need are plastic lenses that offer protection from ultraviolet rays. Why spend a lot of money on a pair of sunglasses that can easily get lost or broken, when the cheapies work just as well?

As soon as you think you've got a sunburn, rub full-strength white vinegar on the exposed areas. Allow the vinegar to soak in for a minute or two before taking a cool shower. The key is to put the vinegar on right away. If you wait until the pain begins, it's too late!

CUT THE LAWN COSTS

Summertime means lawn-mowing season. Use these tricks of the trade to make the job easier and save money.

Keep lawn mower blades sharp. Check them several times during the mowing season and sharpen them at least once a year. Dull mower blades can tear grass instead of making a nice sharp cut, and the tears leave grass more prone to weeds and disease.

Don't cut your lawn too short. Setting your mower blades to leave grass a little higher will encourage strong, deep roots that help keep moisture without having to be watered as often.

Consider a manual mower. Manual mowers are less expensive than gas or electric mowers. They require less maintenance and no electricity, oil, or gasoline. If you have a small yard, it won't take much longer to mow, and you get the added benefit of more exercise.

Never remove more than half the height of the lawn in a single mowing. If rain or an extended vacation has turned your yard into a jungle, adjust the mower blade to cut about half of the height and then wait a couple of days to cut it to the desired height. This saves wear and tear on your mower.

Don't let grass get too tall between mowings. Infrequent mowings are a shock to the grass. You'll end up with more weeds in your lawn.

Take it easy on watering. Not only is water expensive, but a lawn that gets too much water will have more weed problems.

Go Low-Maintenance

When it comes to lawns, low-maintenance means low cost. If you plant your yard and landscape so that you need less water and fertilizer and fewer tools and other accessories, you'll save a significant amount of money. Try some of these low-maintenance, low-cost landscape ideas.

- Shop for disease-resistant or disease-tolerant varieties of trees, flowers, and shrubs.
- In flower beds, plant perennials (flowers that come back year after year) to avoid the yearly task and expense of replanting each year.
- Choose plants, trees, and shrubs that are native to your area. They will thrive during the seasonal weather changes, and you should be able to buy them at bargain prices.
- Buy slow-growing trees and bushes. They will not have to be pruned or fertilized as often.
- Place mulch around all flower beds to hold in moisture and fertilizer.
- Buy the smallest-size tree or shrubs that you can get away with. Smaller trees are almost always cheaper, since the grower will have spent less growing time.

Lawn Fertilizer

Before you go out to buy bags of fertilizer for your lawn, try this low-cost lawn fertilizer. You'll save big money, and the results can be dramatic.

   1 cup Epsom salts
   1 cup household ammonia

Combine in a clean jar. To use, mix 2 tablespoons of the mixture with 2 gallons of water in a watering can and sprinkle over 150 to 200 square feet of turf. Or if you prefer to use a hose sprayer, mix the entire batch with enough water to make one quart of liquid. Pour the liquid into the sprayer. A quart of diluted fertilizer will cover about 2,500 square feet.

Low-Cost Landscaping

You can really save on landscaping if you pick the right plants and flowers. Whereas some plants are expensive and last for just one season or less, many others are just as beautiful and will actually multiply instead of dying off.

- Daisies are a bargain for the price. In two seasons, an inexpensive plant two or three inches tall will grow to fill a square foot of your flower garden with beautiful flowers.

- Buy daffodil bulbs instead of tulips. While tulip bulbs will wither and die off in a few years, daffodil bulbs will multiply and double over time.

- Trade cuttings and seeds with neighbors and friends. Many people are happy to share plant divisions with you in exchange for seedlings or cuttings you may have.

- If you want to make a hedge, choose ilex, Texas sage, or red-tipped Photinia. Small, inexpensive plants are available, and they grow tall and full in just a few years.

- Consider planting fruit trees instead of ordinary shade trees. You'll still get the shade to help lower air conditioning costs, but you'll also get a beautiful tree that can grow in a small space without much care. Your tree could produce bushels of fruit for 20 to 30 years. Dwarf apple trees are low in cost, low in maintenance, and produce lots of apples.

- Buy plants on sale. The biggest sales are at the end of the season. You can find drastic markdowns, because many retailers want to clear out their entire growing stock. If you have a place where you can protect plants until they can safely be planted, you can save a bundle buying at the end of the season.

Also look for end-of-season markdowns on lawn and garden supplies and tools. You may be able to find just what you've been looking for at a very low price.

- Shop garage sales and flea markets for plants and garden tools. You may also be able to find low-cost flowerpots and other accessories.

- Start seeds in egg cartons instead of wasting money on special containers to start seedlings. Use the paper egg cartons. You can plant carton and all.

- Get a soil test from your local agricultural agent or cooperative. By doing this, you'll know exactly what your soil lacks, and you won't waste money on useless additives. The test will be inexpensive—maybe even free. Ask your agent for suggestions on what to add to the soil. The agent will have all sorts of useful free information and is just a phone call away.

Driveway Cleaner

This formula will clean oil, grease, or transmission fluid that has dripped from your car onto a concrete surface. Here's what you'll need:

> Paint thinner
> Cat litter
> Broom

Pour paint thinner straight from the can on the spots. Saturate the spots and an area 6 to 12 inches beyond them. Then spread a thick layer of cat litter over the entire area treated—so thick that you cannot see the concrete surface. Let the cat litter stand for about an hour to absorb the greasy stains. Then use a broom to sweep up the soiled cat litter. Some older stains may require two applications. Be sure to ventilate the area if you are working inside the garage or patio.

SUMMER MOVING

According to statistics from moving companies, an estimated 43 million Americans move every year, more than half of them between May 1 and Labor Day. Before making the big move, plan ahead—you can save hundreds or even thousands of dollars with a little forethought.

If you hire a moving company, one thing you can expect is a big bill. The average household move (transporting around 6,000 pounds a distance of about 1,110 miles) costs more than $4,000 for the movers to pack and move your belongings. But you can shave many of the dollars off with these tips.

Before the Big Move

At your local post office, pick up a copy of an 18-page booklet called *Mover's Guide*. The guide is free, and it includes informative tips, moving-related savings coupons and offers worth more than $60, and change-of-address forms to make sure your mail gets sent to your new address. You'll find coupons for discounts on rental trucks, long distance services, and other moving-related household items.

In advance, arrange to have utilities turned off at the old location and turned on at the new one. If you left a deposit with your present utility company, ask for a refund check. Ask your utility company to write a reference letter to your new utility company stating that you paid your bills on time. With a reference letter on file, many utilities will not make you pay a deposit to have your new service turned on. This is especially true if you move into a small community. Most big-city utility companies will want a deposit regardless of your previous record.

Take your phone books with you. You'll save money by not having to pay for a long-distance directory-assistance call when you need to call someone from the old neighborhood.

Stock up on a few months' worth of any prescription drugs you take. That will cover you until you can find a doctor at your new location.

Plan a garage sale to get rid of the items that you don't want to move to the new location. Price the merchandise to sell. Remember, these are items you don't want to take with you, so you want to get rid of them. Schedule to have a local charity pick up the items that did not sell. No matter whether you move yourself or hire a mover, you'll save money by not moving the stuff you no longer need.

If you are planning a long-distance move, start cleaning out the refrigerator, freezer, and pantry several weeks before the move. Buy the bare minimum at

SAVE ON YOUR MOVE

If you hire a moving company, follow these steps:

1. Do your own packing.
2. Remove mirrors from dressers.
3. Disconnect all appliances.
4. Unplug lamps and remove shades.
5. Disassemble beds.
6. Take down pictures, fans, hanging lamps, and so forth.
7. Move small odds and ends yourself.
8. Have a general idea for the floor plan at the new location so you can quickly direct movers where to put things.
9. Be prepared to help or get out of the movers' way.

MOVING COST		
Average move (1,100 miles)	**3-bedroom house**	**1-bedroom apartment**
You pack	$3,000	$1,500
Movers pack	4,000	1,800
Local move		
You pack	$775	$200
Movers pack	1,375	400

the grocery store. Your aim is to have very few food items to move.

Pack and Save

You can significantly cut your moving bill by packing up your belongings yourself. See the example of typical savings above.

You can save up to half by packing your belongings yourself. But the really big savings can be yours if you are willing to rent or borrow a truck and move your belongings yourself.

Minimize your use of packing material. Instead use the towels, clothing, and linens you are moving anyway to cushion and protect packed items. Pack well enough so that nothing will get broken, but try to add as little extra packing material as possible. If you're using a moving company, not only do you pay for the packing material itself, but also you pay charges by weight and the extra gas used in moving that weight. If you're moving yourself, the extra weight will cut down on your gas mileage.

Expensive items like jewelry and things you need immediately, such as medicines and toiletries, should be carried by you so you can find them more easily.

Time to Save

Try to move on a weekday. Fees can be as much as 50 percent higher on the weekend. If you plan to rent a truck and do the moving yourself, call to reserve a truck. Getting a rental truck on a weekend can be next to impossible, especially near the end of the month.

You Haul It

Renting a truck and doing all the moving yourself can save you thousands of dollars. For a local move, you can rent a truck for 24 hours for less than $100. Many of the truck-rental companies have special prices of $29.95 to $49.95 per day with an additional charge per mile. Call truck-rental companies in your area for the best rate. You'll probably be required to leave a deposit of about $150 on your credit card. When you return the truck, the deposit will be taken off your credit card and the exact amount due will be charged.

LOW-COST LABOR
Hire some neighborhood teenagers to help with the move. Pay them for the day, feed them pizza or burgers for lunch, and you both have a good deal.

If you are planning a local move, you might be able to get away with making several trips in a pickup truck. If you don't have a truck, ask to borrow one from a close friend or relative. If they know you will offer to help with their next move, they will be much more willing to let you use their truck. Return the truck clean and with a full tank of gas. It's a small price to pay for the big savings you will net.

Bargain Boxes

You don't need to pay for boxes for packing; you can get perfect moving boxes free. Grocery stores, printing shops, liquor stores, and office supply stores are all good places to get free boxes. You may have to pick up boxes at night from grocery stores, since most of them stock the shelves at night. Boxes for photocopier paper have lids and are very sturdy. They are great for packing books and other compact items. Arrange to get some from your office, or call a print shop and ask to have some saved for you.

HOME MAINTENANCE AND REPAIRS

Oh, the joys of owning a home—and the costs to maintain and repair it. A homeowner doesn't have the luxury of calling the landlord when a repair is needed. Instead, you must either make the repair yourself or call a service and pay to have the work done. As any homeowner knows, there's always something that needs to be done around the house. Often preventive maintenance will extend the life of an appliance or other part of your home for years. Simple things such as cleaning filters, oiling moving parts, and vacuuming coils are easy ways to cut down on costly repairs. Here are a few examples:

1. Vacuum the coils of your refrigerator. Clean coils allow the refrigerator to operate more effectively, thus using less energy. By keeping the coils clean, you can actually extend the life of your refrigerator by several years.

2. Between washes, turn off the water to your washing machine to reduce stress on the hoses and valves. The stress can lead to broken pipes.

3. Change or clean the air filters on your furnace or air conditioner monthly. This will save energy and reduce the number of repairs.

4. Don't dispose of grease from cooking by pouring it down the drain or garbage disposal. Instead, pour it into a can and put it in the garbage. This simple tip will save you money in plumbers' fees.

5. In general, maintaining your property, house, and furnishings will extend their lives and minimize the need for costly repairs.

Repairs

Even with the best preventive maintenance, the need for repairs around the house will occur. You can save a lot of money if you can handle at least some of the repairs yourself. Many books and videotapes are available at your local library that can walk you through almost any project around the house. Employees at hardware stores are also a great resource for tackling a project yourself. They can answer your questions and let you know if your project can easily be done or if you should call a service technician. Here are some things to keep in mind when you are faced with home repairs.

Learn how to make simple repairs before the breakdown occurs. For example, learn how to relight pilot lights on everything in your house that runs on gas before you have to do it in the cold or without electricity.

Buy a good basic home repair manual and keep it handy. It will quickly pay for itself. You'll find that you can do many projects yourself.

As soon as you move into your new home, locate your power box and learn how to replace a fuse or reset a tripped circuit breaker. It is a good idea to keep a flashlight in an easy-to-find spot, since darkness and tripped breakers tend to go together. When doing any type of electrical work, flip off the circuit breaker or remove the fuse for the area you are working on.

If you are faced with a repair that is over your head, call a qualified service technician. Ask neighbors for advice on who to call. Some companies will give you a free estimate, while others will charge for the estimate but deduct it from the bill if you have the work done. Believe it or not, you may have room to negotiate when given an estimate on a repair. You may feel a little awkward about trying to get an estimate dropped a bit, but remember that it's your money you're spending, and any savings stays in your pocket.

Think twice before you call a repair technician to your house on a weekend or evening. You'll probably pay a premium for these hours. Some companies will even charge extra if they start to work on the job before five o'clock and end up working late. Ask when overtime rates start to make sure you don't pay a premium price.

Home Improvement

If you are planning a major home improvement project or working on the outside of your house, check with the local zoning laws before you start the project. Subdivisions and other parts of the city can have extensive rules and regulations you must follow for any home additions, sheds, carports, driveways, garages, or porches. If you build something that is not allowed, you can be fined and required to tear it down! Even something as simple as a fence can face regulations as to height or nearness to the street.

Remodeling

If you are having a new house built or are doing a major remodeling project, check with your contractors to see if they will reduce the price if you do the cleaning up at the end of the workday. Such jobs as picking up the scraps of wood and sweeping up sawdust are tasks that you can easily do and will save your hired help many hours. Depending on the size of the project, this simple job could save you hundreds of dollars.

PESTS

Summertime means the big invasion of insects. You can end up spending a fortune battling the roaches, ants, and other creepy-crawly or flying pests. Here are some ways to keep the pests away inexpensively.

Those Annoying Ants

Anthills in the yard can be destroyed by pouring a kettle of boiling water down each opening.

To keep ants from coming inside your house, mix two cups of borax with one cup of sugar and sprinkle the mixture around the foundation of the house.

A fairly effective ant stopper for inside the house is ordinary white vinegar. Wash down any areas where you see ants with full-strength vinegar and let the area air-dry.

To keep ants away, the best defense is to not feed them. Keep any crumbs or other small pieces of food wiped up. Ants come into the house looking for food and water. If they can't find what they need, they keep moving.

Ants are also deterred by dried coffee grounds. Sprinkle used coffee grounds outside near the doorways and around any windows.

Ant Traps

These are safe, nonpoisonous traps.

¼ **cup sugar**
¼ **cup baking yeast**
½ **cup molasses**
    Small index cards

Mix sugar, yeast, and molasses in a small bowl. Smear a thin layer of the mixture on each index card with a spatula. Place the cards, syrup side up, in areas where ants travel.

Boric Acid Ant & Roach Bait

1 teaspoon boric acid powder
2½ ounces corn syrup

Mix boric acid powder and corn syrup in a saucepan. Heat over low heat until the boric acid powder completely dissolves. Cool and dilute the mixture with equal parts of water. This will be a sugary, sticky ant and roach bait. Use a spoon or an eyedropper to fill bottle caps or other small containers full of the ant and roach bait. Place the bottle caps where you know roaches or ants have been. You can also use an eyedropper to squeeze the bait into cracks around the foundation of the house inside and outside.

The mixture is poisonous to ants and roaches and remains potent for about three months. Be sure to keep this bait out of the reach of children or pets.

Q. How can I keep meal worms out of my food? It is very expensive to throw the food away when the worms get to it before I do.

A. Meal worms, which are attracted to open packages of macaroni, noodles, or spaghetti, are repelled by the smell of spearmint. You won't be bothered by these pests if you place a few sticks of wrapped spearmint chewing gum in or near the packages. Be sure to leave the gum wrapped so that it won't dry out and lose the spearmint scent.

Picnic Pests

To keep the gnats away while you're outside, rub a thin layer of baby oil on all exposed skin. For mosqui-

> A shilling spent idly by a fool may be picked up by a wiser person.
>
> Benjamin Franklin
> (1706–1790)

toes, rub a little cider vinegar on exposed skin. Both baby oil and vinegar are low-cost ways to keep the pests away.

To kill flying insects, use inexpensive hair spray. The hair spray will harden their wings so they cannot fly. They will literally drop like flies!

Keep ants away from the food on your picnic table by placing each table leg into a bucket or plastic bowl filled with water. The ants cannot swim, so they will leave your picnic food alone!

LIVING ON ONE PAYCHECK

When both parents work, estimates say, an average of 55 to 65 percent of the second income is consumed by work-related expenses. When you add up all the expenses for child care, transportation, parking, work clothing, dry cleaning, and other miscellaneous expenses, you may be surprised to find that staying at home with your children is not an unrealistic goal. You have to be willing to use money-saving strategies to make ends meet, but the good news is you will have more time at home to practice frugality.

Many families have adjusted to living on one paycheck and say the small financial sacrifices are well worth the effort. Parents get to take a more active role in raising their children. Most two-income families spend money on child care and services for lawn care, laundry, and housecleaning. Convenience food products, take-out food, and eating in restaurants are large expenses that can be reduced significantly if one parent is home to plan meals.

Plan Early

If you want to make the transition from two paychecks to one, start planning early—ideally, at least one year before you want to quit working. It will probably take that long to get your savings and finances in order. Start living on one paycheck now. Use the extra paycheck only for work-related expenses such as work clothes, dry cleaning, and transportation. Pay off any credit card debts with whatever is left over. If you do not have any debts, use the money to establish or add to an emergency fund. An emergency fund should have enough money to pay your monthly expenses for at least three months. Before you quit working, your goal should be to have an emergency fund, a savings account, and no debts other than a mortgage.

If you are considering refinancing your mortgage, do it now. It's much easier to qualify for a loan with two incomes. Consider getting a home-equity line of credit approved for emergency money.

Don't cut corners by reducing insurance. Living on one income makes you more vulnerable to financial problems in an emergency. Make sure the wage earner has disability insurance that will equal two-thirds of his or her salary.

Make a Budget

If you have not already done so, make a budget and keep a log of all daily, weekly, monthly, quarterly, and annual expenses. When living on one income, an unexpected or forgotten expense can be devastating!

Haste maketh waste.

John Heywood
(c.1497–c.1580)

Remember that living on one income will take sacrifices. You must be willing to make the necessary lifestyle changes.

Start finding inexpensive or free ways to have fun. Try getting used to a simpler way of life and see if both you and your spouse can enjoy life living on less.

A truly frugal person does not consider shopping a recreational activity. But if you occasionally shop for recreation, it's time to stop. When you are limited to one paycheck, even a few extras each week can wreck your budget.

Part-Time Work

If you find that one paycheck just cannot be stretched to make ends meet, you may want to work part time instead. Working a few evenings a week can bring in some extra income without the added expenses of child care. Some families find that part-time employment is the best solution for everyone. The part-time worker gets to interact with adults and make a little money at the same time, and the other parent gets to spend some time alone with the children.

Reduce Expenses

Whether you are living on one paycheck or just a very tight budget, planning every expense is very important. Taking the time to plan, make phone calls, and search for the best deal can be the best way to enjoy living on less. Try to make saving money fun. Get your whole family involved in the saving and spending process.

Family members will help reduce expenses if they realize there is something in it for them. Saving and planning for a vacation or a special family outing is one of the best ways to get cooperation from children or a reluctant spouse. Children can help by collecting aluminum cans for recycling, clipping coupons, or just remembering to turn out the light when they leave a room. Let the family know how much money must be saved and what they can do to help. Everyone will enjoy the vacation or outing knowing that they did their part to make it possible.

It's important to always keep a positive attitude! If your family hears you complaining that you can't afford this or that, they will start to feel hopeless. Concentrate instead on what you can afford, on all the little pleasures of life. Outings as simple as an afternoon at the park or a picnic can be fun for the entire family.

INDEX

INDEX

INDEX

INDEX

INDEX